D1443308

OLD PEWTER, BRASS, COPPER AND SHEFFIELD PLATE

By courtesy of the Eastman Kodak Company

"I have basins, ewers of tin, pewter, and glass,
Great vessels of copper, fine latten and brass,
Both pots, pans, and kettles such as never was."

1563

OLD PEWTER

BRASS, COPPER, AND
SHEFFIELD PLATE

by N. HUDSON MOORE

with 105 illustrations

CHARLES E. TUTTLE COMPANY
Rutland, Vermont

Representatives
Continental Europe: BOXERBOOKS, INC., *Zurich*
British Isles: PRENTICE-HALL INTERNATIONAL, INC., *London*
Australasia: PAUL FLESCH & CO., PTY. LTD., *Melbourne*
Canada: M. G. HURTIG LTD., *Edmonton*

Published by the Charles E. Tuttle Company, Inc.
of Rutland, Vermont & Tokyo, Japan
with editorial offices at
Suido 1-chome, 2-6, Bunkyo-ku, Tokyo, Japan

Copyright in Japan, 1972, by Charles E. Tuttle Co., Inc.

All rights reserved

Library of Congress Catalog Card No. 75-104206

International Standard Book No. 0-8048-0887-2

First edition published 1905 by Frederick A. Stokes Company, New York
First Tuttle edition published 1972

PRINTED IN JAPAN

TABLE OF CONTENTS

LIST OF ILLUSTRATIONS

Frontispiece (By Courtesy of the Eastman Kodak Co.)

vii

LIST OF ILLUSTRATIONS

Facing Page

PUBLISHER'S FOREWORD

MANY famous collections have been drawn upon to assure the interest of collectors and connoisseurs in this valuable volume on antique metalware. As an example, the author had been able to secure some pieces used by Gen. George Washington at his Mt. Vernon home and in his travels.

The most appealing old pewter is marked by simplicity, good outline and the absence of decoration. It followed three main lines: it was used for church vessels, for household purposes and, to a smaller degree, for civic functions. It is reported to have been known to the ancient Chinese, and the Chaldeans, Egyptians and Greeks claimed to have manufactured it. Its appeal to collectors has grown with the centuries.

Domestic articles in copper and brass in use at the same period as the pewter are also given the full treatment. Splendid collections with the rich appeal of precious metals have furnished the objects used as illustrations.

The first use of brass remains a moot question. History records that a "brazen" bull was cast by Perillus, of Athens, for Phalaris, of Agrigentum, in 570 B.C. It was made hollow, to receive victims who were to be roasted, and the throat was formed to make their groans sound like the bellowings of the animal. It would seem that the Greeks had a lot of brass to treat their victims in such high-handed style.

Sheffield Plate concludes this remarkably handsome reprint on a silver note; several sparkling collections are illustrated in this gem of a book on metal.

PREFACE

OLD pewter is becoming daily of greater interest to the householder, since the fancy for using this attractive ware in country houses has become so widespread. Old plates, platters and chargers that have not seen the light for scores of years, or that have been subjected to indignities, such as covering the flour barrel or catching rain-water leaking into the garret, are now brought forth and treated with pride and consideration.

" Hollow-ware "—jugs, mugs, tankards, and the like— is even more in demand, and if not wanted as ornaments for the shelves in the dining-room, may be used on the table, in appropriate proximity to " Old Blue China " and ancient mahogany, which also have been hauled forth from undeserved obscurity.

Much of the pewter is marked; but in some cases the " touches," as these marks were called, have become almost undecipherable from use. Some of it was made in this country and bears the names of American makers, though much was imported and sold here that had no mark at all. To facilitate the classification of this ware, a list of Continental, English, Scotch and such American names as could be found, has been added to the book; so that in many cases if even part of the name remains, the piece can be identified.

The details of manufacture, the style of decoration, the correct weight of the different pieces of ware are all given. More than a hundred pieces of old ware are illustrated, most of them here reproduced for the first time.

Many famous collections have been drawn upon for this purpose, and the author has been able to secure some pieces in use both at home at Mount Vernon and in the field during Washington's lifetime.

Only one piece of modern pewter is shown; a ewer and basin by M. Jules Brateau, the well-known French sculptor, who is often confused by writers on this subject with Francois Briot, who preceded him by some hundred years.

The household articles in copper and brass in use at about the same period as the pewter are also treated, and as in the case of the latter, splendid collections have furnished the objects used as illustrations. Attention is given to the fancy for the antique Russian articles of these metals, many of which are brought into the country by peasants coming to our shores. These are shown, and the would-be collector is warned of the spurious articles made by the dozen in the dark cellars and back rooms of the East Side, in New York.

Sheffield Plate, a name that has been applied indiscriminately to all old plated ware, is also considered; its manufacture is explained; the manner of identifying it is pointed out; and the names of some of the best known makers are given. Like the other subjects treated in this book, Sheffield Plate is finely illustrated.

PART I

FOREIGN PEWTER

OLD PEWTER, BRASS, COPPER, AND SHEFFIELD PLATE

PART I

FOREIGN PEWTER

WHY is it that old pewter has such a charm? I ask myself again and again why I so admire the few pieces which I own, and why there is such a pleasure in handling them, speculating about them, and in feeling their satiny grey sides,—a feeling not given by any other metal. The very fact that they are so hard to clean calls your attention to them with a persistence that they would not claim if they were susceptible of taking polish quickly, and you rub and rub, and then bend your back and rub again, all too thankful for the slow gleams of silver-like hue which reward your efforts, like the smile on the face of an old friend.

The law of contraries seems operative in regard to the treatment of pewter; for though we restore our china, and have our antiques in the furniture line carefully mended, when we come to our pewter we leave it pretty much alone, with its scratches and batters, its broken-down sides, and the corroded look which so much of it wears. No true lover of this ware will allow his treasures to be burnished, for every time that process is applied to a piece it loses more and more the air of age which was one of its most pleasing allurements, and you might as well have a brand-new piece of modern ware or even of tin.

The use of pewter for household utensils takes it back to the Middle Ages and beyond. Indeed, one cannot go far enough back to find when it was first used in China and Japan,—those lands to which we are bound to turn for so many of the " beginnings of things," and which many of us are pleased to call barbarous countries, because we know no better. So, before examining any of the pewter made in the countries of the West, let us turn to the beautiful specimens which were made hundreds of years ago by those workers who excel in everything that they undertake.

Just how old these pieces are it is impossible to say, yet it is known that pewter ware was made in China two thousand years ago, the composition of the alloy being of lead and tin. There are specimens of Japanese pewter on exhibition in England which are known to be eleven hundred years old, and they are not unlike the pieces presented here, which are on exhibition at the Boston Museum of Fine Arts.

Japanese pewter is often of such a curious tint that it seems impossible to believe that it is pewter. But after an article left the hands of the artisan it was never polished, the only treatment allowed it being a gentle rubbing with a cotton rag. After a time the surface became coated with a faint green rust of two tints,—the lighter forming the ground, and

Fig. 1. CHINESE PEWTER
Boston Museum of Fine Arts

the darker showing in mottled patches,—which gave it a very artistic appearance, but which must have been unpleasant to eat from, I should think.

In general the vessels were not flat, but hollow ware, and some of them were modelled from the ever-present form of the lotus, and some of them bear the figure of Buddha the Mysterious.

The pewter used by the Japanese contains so much lead that it was susceptible of much working, and in some of the illustrations shown, the familiar dragon is on guard. A harder and more brittle quality of pewter, containing a large proportion of antimony, was also made by them, and this was admirably adapted for casting or stamping in intricate and delicate forms. Occasionally a piece is found which has been coated with some other metal, but in many cases the coating is carelessly done and flakes off.

Both Japanese and Chinese use engraving as a form of decoration, and the grace and simplicity of the patterns employed do credit, as usual, to their innate love of beauty, and present a marked contrast to the patterns employed by other nations working at the same period. The Chinese added to the decorative appearance of pewter by introducing both copper and brass in various patterns, as can be seen in Figures 2 and 3. The grotesque figure bearing a basket is entirely of pewter.

The composition of pewter varies, not only in the different countries where it was made, but also as regarded the purpose for which it was designed. Below is given a slight table, showing not only the ingredients which entered into the composition of the metal, but the proportions used.

	Tin	Lead	Antimony	Copper
Plate Pewter, best quality	100	. . .	8	4
Plate Pewter, poorest quality	89.3	. . .	7.1	1.8
Common Pewter, "Trifle"	82	. . .	18	
Tin and Temper	100	. . .	. . . . .	26
Pewter, called "better" . .	56	8	. . . . .	6
Pipe Metal	60	40		
Metal for Salts and Ewers .	90	10		
Metal for dishes, etc. . . .	96	4		
Ley Metal	80	20		

Tin, which has always been the metal entering most largely into the composition of pewter, has from an early period played an important part in the manufacture of domestic utensils. The Egyptians used it as early as 3700 B.C., and it is mentioned at least twice in the Bible, and also by Plautus and Pliny. The English pewterers drew their supply of tin chiefly from the Cornish mines, and the output averaged about 8,000 tons per annum. Lead, another component part of pewter, was also drawn from places near the tin mines, and England was known as the " classic land of lead and tin." Herodotus speaks of the trade in lead as the chief inducement which brought the Phœnicians to the shores of Britain, and a writer on the subject of lead says:

Fig. 2.　CHINESE PEWTER VASE
Boston Museum of Fine Arts

"These two metals [tin and lead] made the early fame of Britain; they brought here the Phœnician trader, and had doubtless much to do with the Roman occupation of this distant island."

The Romans used pewter for seals of office, and some years ago there were many of them to be found in the county of Westmoreland, England, left there by the Roman legions. They were of all shapes, round, oval, or rectangular, and it is a pity that, owing to their making excellent solder, they have been entirely destroyed by the enterprising tinkers of the neighbourhood.

For use at home, the Romans carried tin from Cornwall both by ship and overland, and when material for the proper alloys failed them, they made pewter of pure tin. The metals were transported in the form of ingots, and not only did Rome get her share, but France too, received her quota, by means of either caravan or boat. Holland got hers through the city of Bruges; and Barcelona sent out so much to Venice and other parts of Italy that it was found necessary to regulate the trade, and as early as 1406 the first of these regulating statutes was framed.

The word "Pewter" has its equivalents in many languages, *peautre* dating from 1229 in France, while the Dutch used *speawter,* or *peawter,* and in old English inventories I find it spelled in half a score of ways, according to the fancy and degree of education of the writer.

The French, ever more elegant and refined than the English in matters relating to household furnishing and domestic utensils, had fine pewter in their homes before it was made in England. By 1390 not only the nobles, but the wealthy ecciesiastical dignitaries had large supplies of pewter plate, and in 1401, Isabeau of Bavaria, wife of Charles VI of France, bought for her kitchen nine dozen dishes and twenty-three porringers. This queen, whatever view you may take of her morals, may at least have the credit for introducing many improvements into palaces, which had hitherto been bare and cheerless enough. Among the existing records of items of expenditure for herself and her household are charges for the "making of a large box of wood and iron, with holes in it, to burn a candle by night in the room of Madame Jehanne." This was the first approach to a night-lamp, and "Madame Jehanne" was one of the younger princesses.

Isabeau at this same time had made for her use great baths of oak, and she was the first one to use a "suspended carriage." Those vehicles, which were made under her direction, were elegant and luxurious to a degree never seen before, and had four wheels. She had heaters made in the form of little iron chariots, which were filled with red-hot ashes and were wheeled about her rooms to warm them. She also had made balls of gold or silver, to be filled with ashes and held in the hand for warmth. Although she bought much pewter for her kitchen, her own personal plate was gold, and as a charm against poison she used an Eastern talisman which was chained with a silver-gilt chain to her goblet and saltcellar. She did not place such entire reliance on this talisman as

Fig. 3. CHINESE PEWTER
Boston Museum of Fine Arts

Fig. 4. JAPANESE PEWTER AND CHINESE PEWTER JUG
Boston Museum of Fine Arts

might at first appear, since, despite its supposed efficacy, she had every dish of which she partook tasted by an officer of her household before it approached her lips.

In 1500, in Paris, it was stated that the necessary number of pewter dishes for a state dinner was six dozen large porringers, the same number of small plates, two and a half dozen large dishes, eight quart and twelve pint tankards, and two dishes for scraps for the poor.

The period of the most showy development of pewter began in France about 1550, and François Briot was its most celebrated worker. Originally a maker of dies and moulds, he became a worker in metals, and wrought with the greatest success in soft alloys. Examples of his work are to be seen in many of the museums of Europe, and his most noted production was a flagon and salver, with figures, emblems, masks, and strap-work. These elegant pieces were cast in sections, joined together, and then finished in the most careful manner in delicate relief.

Jules Brateau, a modern French sculptor, has used pewter in somewhat the same manner as his predecessor, Briot, and in Figure 6 is shown an example of his work which may be seen at the Chicago Museum of Fine Arts. Like the work of Briot, it consists of a salver and ewer, and the salver contains in the centre a large round boss on which is a winged globe, the symbol of Fame. About this boss a line of Cupids disport themselves, bearing a ribbon on which are inscribed the names of those celebrated in the arts of

Music, Painting, Sculpture, and Architecture. The body of the salver has four panels, with figures representing the above-mentioned arts, each panel being separated from those on either hand by the tools and emblems of the various arts and crafts. The rim is moulded with a scroll border, which is lightened by the introduction of flower-buds at certain places in the design.

The ewer has for a handle a nude female figure holding a mirror, and the body of the vessel is decorated with seated female figures representing Science, Literature, and the Drama. The base of the ewer is hardly in keeping with the rest of the composition, which on the whole compares favourably with the work of the earlier master. M. Brateau has chosen for his "touch" the singular device of a gallows with two rows of figures hanging thereon!

François Briot was followed by Gaspar Enderlein, a Swiss, and by 1600 the Nuremberg workers entered the field with richly worked plates and platters,— those with religious subjects being used as patens, while those with secular designs were for ornament on the heavily carved dressers of the middle classes, in imitation of the collections of gold and silver plate which were displayed by the wealthy nobles. These ornate pieces, if of French origin, were called by the specious name of " A facon d'argent," and, like the modern "art novelties" from the same source, brought good prices.

During the century from 1680 to 1780 much pewter was made in France, though the greater part of it

Fig. 5.   JAPANESE PEWTER, ENGRAVED DECORATION
Boston Museum of Fine Arts

Fig. 6.   MODERN FRENCH PEWTER BY JULES BRATEAU
Chicago Museum of Arts

was made in the first three-quarters of that time. Louis XVI appointed a royal pewterer, and he made the nobles give up to him much of their silver plate. To make the use of pewter more satisfactory, he granted special permission that it might be adorned with gold or lacquer, which privilege had hitherto been given exclusively to the dignitaries of the Church. As in England, French workmen had been gathered into guilds or corporations, but these were abolished by Turgot on the ground that the free right to labour was a sacred privilege of humanity. With the dispersion of the guilds the quality at least of the pewter declined, and, though it kept its place among the middle classes, with the wealthy its use was relegated to the kitchen. Then, too, after 1750, the use of pottery and porcelain gradually increased, and the beauty of these wares made them easily favourites.

As a proof of their skill the French workmen had to make a piece of the ware of the class to which they belonged, before they could be admitted to the Guild. They were divided into special classes as early as the fourteenth century, and the "*potiers d'étain*" consisted of three classes: those who made vases, "*potiers dit de rond*," then those who made the hammered ware and had to present a dish or bowl as a specimen of their work, and were known as "*les potiers maître de forge*," and lastly the "*potiers menuisiers*," who made little things like pilgrims' and beggars' badges, toys for children, rings and buttons, and who had to make for their entrance piece an inkstand or a salt-cellar.

Many of the rules which governed the French pewterers were substantially the same as those which were in force in England. In fact the French claim that the English pewterers took their regulations as the model on which they framed their own rules of the Pewterers' Company. In 1613 Louis XIII gave a set of statutes to the French pewterers, at the same time that he gave a set to the Guild of Armourers. Before a man was qualified to become a master workman, he was obliged to serve an apprenticeship of six years, to serve three years as a journeyman, and then make his admission piece. The sons of masters were exempt from serving an apprenticeship, provided that they worked three years with their father. They did not have to make an admission piece and they did not have to pay dues.

As in England, each pewterer had to have his private mark, which was registered with the King's Procurer as well as in the guild room. Each master had two marks, the larger containing the first letter of his Christian name and the whole of his surname, while the smaller mark gave only the initials of both names. Besides this, each mark contained the device of the master, the choice of which was left to his own fancy.

Works in the common metal were marked on the upper side; works of high quality, antimony, tin, or of resonant metal, were marked on the lower side. Saltcellars, small measures, and little articles were to have ten per cent of lead, while small plates and saucers were to have but four per cent.

Fig. 7. FRENCH ANTIQUE PUNCHED WORK
Collection of Mrs. Charles Barry

According to Boileau the regulations for the Paris pewterers were as follows:

"1. Whatever persons wish to be pewterers in Paris may be so without restriction, if only they do good and lawful work. They may have as many workmen and apprentices as they may wish.

"2. No pewterer may work at night, or upon a festival day. Whoever does so will have to pay a fine of five sols, to the King. The light at night is not enough for him to do good and lawful work.

"3. No pewterer may or should by law work at any work of his trade which is not well and lawfully alloyed according to the requirements of the work. If he does so he forfeits the work and incurs a fine of five sols to the King.

"4. No coppersmith nor other person may sell wares belonging to the pewterers' trade, either in the town or outside, nor in his house, unless it is of good and legal alloy. If he does so he must forfeit the work and pay a fine of five sols, to the King.

"5. No one may or ought to sell wares belonging to the pewterers, or is to sell old pewter as new. If he does he must pay a fine of five sols, to the King.

"6. The masters of the pewterers require that two experienced masters of the trade be elected by order of the Provost of Paris. The said masters are to swear solemnly that the men of the said trade will keep the above regulations, well and loyally.

"7. The pewterers are liable to serve on the watch if they are under sixty years of age.

"8. The two experienced masters, elected as above, are exempt from serving on the watch.

"9. The pewterers are to pay taxes and other dues, as paid by the other citizens of Paris to the King."

The master pewterers were allowed to make all kinds of work provided that they used fine and resonant pewter, alloyed with copper and bismuth. It was, however, forbidden that they should use either gold or silver on their pewter ware, except such as was intended for use in churches. Patens and chalices were always to be of the best quality, and this was a rule which was carried out in all countries. Master pewterers were not to begin work with the hammer before five in the morning, nor to continue it after eight in the evening. Nor were they allowed to put on sale in their shops any pewter which was not made by a Parisian pewterer in Paris. Widows were allowed to continue the business of their husbands, and to keep open shop as long as they continued widows.

In 1776 the guilds of pewterers, coppersmiths, and scalemakers were all combined, and from this time on the industry of pewter-making slowly and steadily declined.

Some of the best French pewter is marked " *blanc*," which indicates its superior quality; the bluer the colour, the more lead in its composition.

French pewter does not seem to have been held in such high esteem as that made in Germany or the Netherlands. In 1709 various foreign pewters were tested at Pewterers' Hall in London, French and Spanish showing from $14\frac{1}{2}$ to 29 less than "fine," while a piece of English pewter taken at random from a shop was but $1\frac{1}{2}$ grains less than fine, or the standard quality. No doubt the inferior quality was because the manufacture was very general all over France, and because the corporation was not so "close" as in England.

Lyons was known abroad for its excellence in pewter ware by 1295, and Paris had Gautier at work as early as 1300, while other less famous names were

Fig. 8. GERMAN CAVALRY CUP
Collection of Mr. Browne

Robert (1313); Guillaume de Liloies (1315): Adan l'Escot; Huguein de Besançon (1531), pewterer to the royal household; Michelet Breton (1580), also purveyor to the house of the king; and in 1401 we find the name of Jehan de Montrousti, who furnished the kitchen ware for Isabeau of Bavaria, already mentioned.

In Poitiers, Limoges, Tours, Amiens, Rouen, Dijon, as well as in Montpellier, Angers, Bordeaux, Toulouse, and in many other cities, there were pewterers at work early in the fourteenth century. In the ornamentation of pewter the French excelled in engraved work, though they had a fancy for figures in high relief, which were either cast solid, or punched out from the back and then filled in with lead. The plates shown in Figure 7 have the edge moulded on afterward by hand, and they are further ornamented by engraving. One has a coat of arms, while the other is merely decorative. Such pieces were of course never used on the table, but were for ornament only on the wall or dresser.

Badges or tokens of pewter were favourite relics of pilgrims, to show that they had actually made a pilgrimage. The shape of a cockle-shell in memory of St. Michel was the usual device, and pilgrims wore these in their hats by the twelfth century. In the Cluny Museum at Paris is an old mould for casting such badges, and this one is in the shape of a heart, with a cross and the letters I.H.S. In no country did the custom of wearing these tokens prevail to a greater extent than in France; indeed some authorities contend that it originated there. St. Denis was the favourite saint in the north, while in the south St. Nicholas prevailed. There were, besides, many local saints, of which little images were cast, and these were worn on hat or coat.

Mont St. Michel was the chief place for the distribution of these badges, and it is said that the cockleshells found on the beach there served for the first models. A thriving business was done in these badges, and by the fourteenth century it was brought to the notice of the king, who thereupon imposed a tax on these articles. This called forth so loud a protest from the pewterers that the king, Charles VI ("the Well-Beloved"), exempted these badges from all tax for ever. Such badges, brought home from a pilgrimage, had an honoured place in the house, and were pointed to with reverence and pride by their owners.

Little vessels for containing holy-water or the oil of extreme unction were also made of pewter, and sometimes made long journeys to the Holy Land on the persons of the devout, who brought home in them various kinds of sacred relics, a little dust from Calvary, or, if the pilgrimage had been made to Rome, some earth from the Catacombs. These little bottles or relic-holders had wide mouths, and were closed by pressing their lips hard together. They were then hung on a string and suspended from the neck.

An interesting relic found during the last century was enclosed in a box made of a material which was called lead, but which was actually composed of lead mixed with some harder metal which gave it more

Fig. 9. GERMAN TANKARD
Collection of Mrs. George Brodhead

Fig. 10. GERMAN SOUP TUREEN
Cooper Union Museum, New York

body and durability. In the fine cathedral of Rouen, France, is a suite of four rooms containing what is known as the " *Trésor*." This collection of very valuable and interesting relics forms quite a little museum, and may be seen upon the payment of a small fee. To an Anglo-Saxon the most notable object in the collection is the so-called leaden casket in which was buried the heart of the famous King, Richard Cœur de Lion, who was slain by a bolt from the crossbow of Bertrand de Gourdon at the siege of the castle of Chaluz. His body lies at the feet of his father at Fontevrault, near Tours, but his heart, encased in two leaden caskets, was buried in the cathedral at Rouen, " the faithful city." The exact place of its burial seems to have been forgotten in the lapse of years, but it was rediscovered in 1840, put in a new casket, and once more buried in its old resting-place in the choir. The old leaden cases, the outer one of which was much corroded, were placed in the " *Trésor*," or treasure-chamber, and on one is to be seen this inscription:

Cercueil
et
Boite de Plomb
ou fut renfermé
lors de sa sepulture en 1199
le Cœur de
RICHARD CŒUR DE LION
Trouvés en 1840
dans le sanctuaire de la Cathédral
de Rouen.

The inner casket, after all these centuries of time, is still in good condition, the inscription it bears being perfectly legible. The Latin is quaint enough, and though the art of working on metals was quite advanced at that time, and rare and beautiful objects were wrought, the man selected to do this piece of work could not have been a skilled workman, even if his casket was to hold the heart of the mightiest king on earth. He worked so ill that he did not leave room enough on the line to put the whole of the king's name, but had to carry over one letter to the next line. Richard's title is given as " Regis Anglorum," King of the English, while no mention is made of either Normandy or Aquitaine. The inner box is about a foot long, eight inches wide, and five inches deep. The fashion of burying the heart was a not unusual one, for in those days it was well-nigh impossible to transport the body to some loved spot; but the heart, a small thing, could be brought home, from even the scenes of the Crusades, and laid to rest where its onetime owner desired.

A less romantic but also interesting article which is occasionally met with in museums is a " *cymaise,*" a kind of drinking-cup. These were in use as early as 1370, when mention is made of some of them in the inventory of the Bishop of Troyes. When any dignitary came to visit a city, were he of the Church or State, it was customary for a deputation of the nobles of the town to go out and meet him and offer him wine, the attendants of the visitor receiving as a perquisite the cup from which the wine was drunk. These great cups were frequently made of pewter, fitted with two handles, one for grasping the vessel when the

Fig. 11. GERMAN TANKARDS AND JUG
Collection of Mrs. Charles Barry

Fig. 12. GERMAN PEWTER, ENGRAVED AND WRIGGLED
WORK
Collection of Mrs. Charles Barry

liquor was taken to the mouth, the other a swinging handle fastened near the top of the cup. The fixed handles were plain and solid, while the swinging ones were very richly ornamented. Such cups were also offered as prizes for feats of skill, and when given at shooting contests bore, besides the name of the town, a bow and arrow or a gun. This old custom holds good to-day, and the prizes at Oxford and Cambridge for rowing contests are still called " pewter pots," though now they are only Britannia metal.

In Germany the chief places where pewter was made were Nuremberg and Augsburg, records of enactments at the latter place showing that the pewterers' workshops were inspected by the masters of the craft as early as 1324. Nuremberg had her famous workers too,—at this time Carel, and Sebaldus Ruprecht being among the best known. One of the earliest ordinances regulating the making of pewter in Nuremberg is dated 1576. In this it is expressly stated that pewterers were forbidden to make anything with English tin or beaten tin, only pure tin being recognised, without the addition of any lead. Such articles as were made according to these regulations could be marked with an eagle and a crown, while those which were made after the English fashion were to have, in addition to the eagle and crown, a rose as well.

Each member of the craft had to make a sample plate and have it approved by the master craftsmen, after which he was allowed to punch it with his private mark, which consisted of the eagle (the town mark), in the field of which he added his own device. The plate so marked might then be hung in some public place where his mark could be seen and noted, so that his ware could be recognised by those who had it in use in their households. Apparently this was as near as it was allowed for merchants to advertise their wares. The ordinance closes with this order:

"The masters must go at least four times a year into all workshops, cellars, and shops, to see if the alloy is pure. If they find in their inspection defects in work caused by careless casting or bad turning, the article is to be broken up, and if the pieces weigh more than half a pound the owner of the workshop is to pay a fine of one twelfth. If the pieces exceed half a pound in weight, they are to be put into the melting-pot."

A fine example of one of the great flagons or drinking-vessels is shown in Figure 8. It is of German manufacture, and an inscription on the front shows that it belonged to a German cavalry regiment, though there is no date. The figure on the top is a cavalry officer in uniform, and it is to be regretted that there is no maker's mark. This style of flagon was familiar in the seventeenth century, and they were extremely heavy, from twenty-five to thirty pounds being not uncommon. The pewter was made of great thickness in parts, and, as they were almost too bulky to pass around, a tap was often added later. The one on the cavalry cup is more ornamental than useful, and in keeping with the cherubs' heads which answer for feet. This piece is twenty-two inches high and in excellent condition, although the cherubs' noses are somewhat battered.

A small and more modern drinking-tankard, six

Fig. 13. FLEMISH PEWTER, MARKED "GHENT"
From the Collection of Mr. Browne

inches high, simple in form, and with a fine thumb-piece, is shown in Figure 9. It has a splendid maker's mark on the inner side,—a crowned figure standing in a circle.

I have found only one soup-tureen; it is of German make, and is shown in Figure 10. The mark on the bottom is much worn, but the piece may be seen at the Museum of Cooper Union, New York. The bowl is fine in shape, moulded in panels, and stands in a tray, also moulded in panels, and rather deep. The quality of the pewter is excellent and readily takes a high polish.

Two German tankards and a pitcher are shown in Figure 11, all of good workmanship. The smallest tankard bears within the name of Ruprecht, which was famous among pewter-workers in the fourteenth century, though this piece is not so old, of course. It is, however, one of the old types, before the lids began to rise, the modern tankard having a bell-shaped lid, years adding successive degrees of height till they were often several inches high. This lid has a medallion set in the top,—a favourite form of decoration, a coin sometimes being used instead of the medallion. The second tankard is of rather unusual shape, the bottom looking more like a pitcher than a tankard. It is dated 1789 on the ornamental band which goes around the top. This kind of ornament was known as "wriggled" or "joggled" work. Owing to the character of the alloy, engraved work wears out very quickly, since it has to be very lightly done. as deeply cut work weakens the ware. The tool which makes the wriggled work is of the nature of a chisel, the blades being of varying width, the common size measuring about an inch. The pattern is impressed on the object by rocking or joggling the tool along, and although this work is found on the pewter of all countries, the German and Dutch pewterers seem to have had a particular preference for it. The Dutch put much of it on pewter for church use, covering the chalice or flagons with long stories from the Bible, the quaint figures having below them a few words to indicate what they are intended to represent. For such purposes the tool may be as fine as one thirty-second of an inch broad. A running pattern is often chosen for secular vessels, and the lines seem to be composed of dots, as on the tankard, but on close inspection the connecting line can be discovered.

On the little pitcher with the wooden handle, a small beading is seen around the lid, produced by a stamping or milling process.

In Figure 12 is shown some handsome work done with an engraver's tool. In this work some of the pewter is removed with each stroke of the tool, and a tracing-tool is used besides, the graver making the deeper lines. All three of these pieces have elaborate coats of arms on them, and the bowl is plainly marked " Graf von Ehren, 1735." They all are marked with the rose and crown, which is found on Dutch, German, French, Flemish, and Scotch as well as English ware, though the idea is prevalent that the mark is exclusively English. I would feel inclined to say that the

Fig. 14. EIGHTEENTH-CENTURY BENITIER, FLEMISH

lip on the beaker had been added later, but on it are to be found some of the maker's marks.

The use of the graver can always be distinguished from the tracing-tool by the appearance of the ornament. The graver removes some metal with every stroke, while the tracing-tool is held in a vertical position and is struck with a mallet, a small portion of the alloy being displaced and standing up on each side of the pattern, like a furrow. As the pattern progressed, the tool was moved along in the proper direction and was regularly struck with the mallet, and if the object on which the ornament is applied be examined with a magnifying-glass, the marks of the mallet may be plainly seen. To make this style of ornamentation there were curved punching-tools as well as straight ones, but if the decorator were a man of skill he could produce nearly all his effects with the straight tool.

Another form of ornament was called "pricked" work, and presents a similar appearance to the wriggled ornament. It was often finished with a slight engraved line on either side of it, and if kept to severe and simple curves was not a bad ornamentation.

Pewter at its best is plain, relying for its pleasing appearance on its form, on the quality of the alloy, and on its colour. Some of the Corporation or Guild cups are very handsome, being tall, stately vessels, the simple lettering in script, either on the body of the cup or on a shield, being all that was necessary. There were many calls, however, for more elaborate work, and there were masters of the craft who wrought in this simple metal in what we must confess was a pleasing style.

Many of the European museums and some of America have specimens of this ancient cast and worked pewter, and the Nuremberg Museum, besides the collections in the lower halls, which consist of splendid cups and tankards which belonged to Guilds and Corporations, has in the upper story a kitchen furnished after the fashion of the seventeenth century. Here may be studied many wonderful examples of domestic articles in pewter, as well as some which were used on state occasions only. These articles are so arranged that the visitor has every opportunity to study them, and it is a way vastly superior to placing them in cases, where it is impossible to see more than one side of an object, and never the markings.

Figure 13 is a salver or tray which measures ten inches in diameter, with a good rococo border of carved and pierced work. It is marked on the back, "Ghent," and the maker's name is plainly stamped in two places, "Charnold Lucas," in an oval-shaped touch-mark, the name coming at the bottom, while on the upper side of the oval are the words, "Fin blok Zin." In the centre of the touch is the figure of an angel with a sheaf in its hand, and somewhat abbreviated garments, as the feet are plainly to be seen. It is not the figure of St. Michel, which was sometimes used by the Ghent pewterers, though it was the Brussels mark also. The Lucases were well-known English pewterers, Robert Lucas being a

Fig. 15. SWISS PLATE
Boston Museum of Fine Arts

master in 1667, and Stephen being one as late as 1824. Charnold Lucas must have been one of the family who settled in Ghent and carried on his business there, and very beautiful work he did too, treating the material as if it were silver. The fine scalework in portions of the pattern is worthy of note.

At the Museum of Ghent there is a touch-plate of the Ghent pewterers of the seventeenth and eighteenth centuries. The commonest mark was the rose and crown, with the initials of the maker placed just below the crown or even in it. There was another mark which seems to have been an equal favourite, and that was a small hammer having on either side of its handle a shield, one bearing a lion, and the other a lamb with a flag. A crown is placed above the whole device.

There are still workers at the pewterer's trade in Ghent, the most famous being members of the De Keghels family. There is a touch-plate at Ghent which shows many of the ancient family marks, among them being the rose and crown of course, with the initial letters sometimes going across the rose, but more often in the crown. Another mark of this family was an oval containing a fleur-de-lys and the letters I. D. K. Then there are a Maltese cross within a circle, a sheep in an oblong, a heart in an oval, a heart pierced with two arrows, and—perhaps the handsomest mark of all—a lion within a circle.

The Flemish workers in pewter often produced works of great delicacy and beauty, and did not confine its use to domestic utensils and corporation pieces.

They also used it for church vessels, although this was protested against very strongly by the Roman Catholic Church on the ground that pewter was not sufficiently precious metal from which to fashion sacred vessels. In 847 the Council of Rheims, and in the thirteenth century the Synod of Canterbury, forbade its use for making the paten and chalice. In 1252, at Nismes, these two decisions were confirmed, but poor communities were permitted to continue the use of their pewter vessels. Even at the present day in Belgium the Eucharistic vessels for every-day use are made of pewter, and down to the times of the Revolution in France it was the custom to reserve the vessels of precious metal for special services and great occasions.

You may find to-day hanging in Flemish churches the *bénitier,* or Holy-Water cup, and it may be made of pewter, though it will not be so ornate or finely wrought as the one shown in Figure 14, which was made in the eighteenth century. It is fashioned with almost the fineness of silver, and so carefully finished after it was removed from the mould that it looks almost like hand-work. These small articles were sometimes hung beneath the shrines at the wayside, but most of them were much cruder objects than this one.

One of the most famous examples of cast-work is shown in Figure 15. It is a plate, or *Kaiserteller,* eight inches in diameter, with a border of thirteen lobes, each one displaying the arms of one of the Swiss Cantons. It is presumably of Swiss workmanship and

Fig. 16. KAISERTELLER, FERDINAND III
Boston Museum of Fine Arts

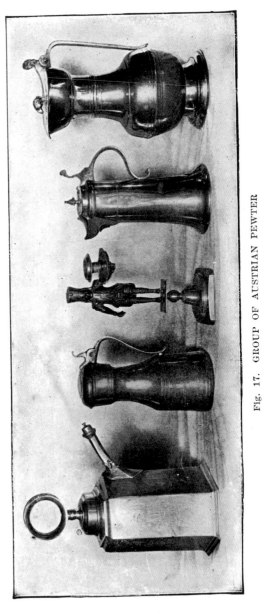

Fig. 17. GROUP OF AUSTRIAN PEWTER

is dated 1508. Between the three upper lobes, lettered Bern, Zurich, and Lucern, may be distinguished three shields. These bear, first the letter G; next a monogram made up of the letters I. S.; and then a merchant's mark. T. Z. which is repeated on the back. Around the medallion in the centre is the legend:

"DO . MAN . 1508 . ZELT . DER . ERSTE . PUNDT . WARD . VON . GOTERWELT."

The alloy is extremely soft and has suffered somewhat, as may be seen, but in the main the plate is in excellent preservation, considering its age, though it has been used for ornament only.

Another very choice piece of pewter is the plate shown in Figure 16. This specimen is some of the famous Nuremberg work, and has for its central medallion the figure of Ferdinand III. On the border are the six Electors, with their coats of arms. On the back is the date 1645, and between the 16 and the 45 is the letter S pierced by an arrow. In another place are the letters I. G. L. This, like the previous plate, is of extremely soft alloy, but still shows its fine work. The excellence of the moulds in which such show-pieces were cast left little work to be done when the castings were removed.

PART II

ENGLISH AND AMERICAN PEWTER

PART II

ENGLISH AND AMERICAN PEWTER

THE use of pewter for utensils of the household succeeded wood, and their manufacture had become of sufficient importance in England by the end of the thirteenth century to be mentioned in official documents. By 1290 King Edward I had "leaden" vessels for cooking the boiled meats for the coronation feast, and had a supply of over three hundred pewter dishes, salts, and platters in his possession. He seems to have had no silver plate at all.

In the "Rolls of Parliament" there is a curious document called "State of the Poor," and in this are given some valuations of furniture and stock in trade of some of the merchants of Colchester, England, for the year 1296. A carpenter's stock was valued at one shilling, and consisted of five tools only. The lists of the other tradesmen were almost as small; the only one which exceeded one pound in value was that of a tanner, whose stock was estimated at £9 7s. 10d., showing that his was the principal trade, a fact which is easily understood, as the chief part of men's dress was leather. Most of the lesser cities drew upon London for their necessaries, and the lists of household goods among even the nobles were wonderfully poor and mean. Some hundreds of years later Harrison wrote a " Description of England in Shakespeare's Youth," in which he says:

" It has mines of gold, silver, and tin (of which all manner of table utensils are made, in brightness equal to silver and used all over Europe), of lead and iron alsoe, but not much of the latter. . . . Tin and lead, mettals which Strabo noteth in his time to be carried unto Marsilis from hence, the one in Cornewall, Devonshire (and elsewhere in the north), the other in Darby Shire, Weredale, and sundrie places of this Island; whereby my countrymen doo reap no small commoditie, but especiallie our pewterers, who in time past imploied the use of pewter onlie upon dishes, pots, and a few other trifles for use here at home, whereas now they are growne unto such exquisite cunning that they can in manner imitate by infusion anie fashion or forme of cup, dish, salt bowle, or goblet, which is made by goldsmith's crafts, though they be never so curious, exquisite, and artificiallie forged."

Tin by itself is not so durable and ductile as lead, and the two metals combined will not shrink so greatly as either taken separately, a quality which had to be considered when the object under consideration had to be cast in a mould. Because of its fusibility pewter was much used by goldsmiths to take the first castings of medals or other objects, so that they could be shown to customers for approval. Benvenuto Cellini is known to have used pewter for obtaining the first proofs of his medals and coins, and also used it to make his bronze flow more easily.

The earliest pewter of best quality was made of tin with as much brass as the tin could take up, the proportion being about four to one. In this quality, which was called " fine," were made many small articles like salts, cruets, pitchers, also platters, chargers and church vessels. A less fine quality consisted of tin and lead, and the proportion here was also four to one. This alloy was used for candlesticks, bowls, and pots. The tankards and mugs used in public houses had a still greater proportion of lead, and were sometimes known as "black metal," because they tarnished so easily. The composition of Japanese pewter of the seventeenth and eighteenth centuries is almost identical with the second quality of pewter already spoken of,—that is, about one to four of lead and tin.

It is impossible to tell easily, and without applying a chemical test, how much lead a piece of pewter contains. If you pass a piece of pewter across a bit of white paper, the presence of lead will be indicated by a dark mark,—the greater the amount of lead the darker the mark. If there is as much as ninety parts of tin to ten of lead, there will be no mark, but seventy-five per cent of tin, and twenty-five of lead will give a faint mark. Between these two points it is all guesswork, and with less than seventy-five per cent of tin all pewter will give this mark.

The methods of making pewter have always been the same, and it depended upon the nature of the object whether it was cast, or hammered, or both, and then finished by being put upon a lathe and burnished.

The most necessary thing for a pewterer was a set of moulds, and as these were made, if possible, of gun-metal, they were costly and could not be easily obtained. Probably this was one reason for the gathering of the pewterers into guilds or fellowships, for in that case the moulds were owned by the company and were loaned or rented to members, some guilds, like those at York, England, making a special rule that the moulds were to be loaned without charge to the members.

Although pewter was sometimes cast in sand or in moulds of plaster-of-paris or metal, the best moulds, as already stated, were of gun-metal. These were fitted with wooden handles for convenience in lifting, and after a pewter object was taken from the mould it was made bright by polishing. If possible, the article was cast in one piece, and this was the case with small objects, such as spoons, small salts, porringers, bleeding-dishes, etc. When it came to large ewers, or tankards with bulging sides, it was necessary to cast the piece in sections, solder them together, and then finish them off, but it is almost always possible to detect the joints. Tankards with straight sides were also cast in three pieces, and in some the bottom was made of glass, so that the customer could keep an eye as to the quality of liquor he was getting. If the handles were hollow, they were cast in two pieces, joined, and then soldered to the body of the tankard.

Plates, properly made, were first cast and then hammered, four or five rows of hammer-marks showing on the under side. The hammering gave strength to the metal and a good finish. This rule, however, applies solely to the smaller sizes of plates, for large platters, or chargers, were made entirely with the hammer from rolled sheets of metal. It was the ancient custom to fashion small dishes or bowls with

Fig. 18. KITCHEN AT MOUNT VERNON

"ears" all in one piece, and those pewterers who made the ears separately and soldered them on were reprimanded if the fact were discovered by the company. Saltcellars were either cast in a mould and then hand-finished, or cast in two pieces, then soldered, and finished. This is usually the case with those which have a foot.

The tools used by the pewterer were comparatively simple and few in number. After the moulds, the lathe was the most important implement. It consisted of a head-stock and a tail-stock, with a simple mandrel, the motive power being supplied by a boy or an unskilled workman, who was called a "turn-wheel." Then came, in order of value, the hammer, the anvil, chisels, gouges, hooks, and the tools used in burnishing. Notwithstanding that the lathe was considered a tool in the pewterers' craft, its use was restricted, and an edict dated 1595 enacts that no saucers shall be sold save those which are beaten with hammers.

The most valuable records of the English pewterers and their craft are contained in the books of "The Worshipful Company of Pewterers," which go back as far as 1348,—about the middle of the reign of Edward III. The Company is described as the "Craft of Pewterers," and the ordinances deal exclusively with matters relating to the trade. These records, which contain the history of the Company down to 1760, have recently been transcribed,—a task of almost unending difficulty, which has been accomplished by Mr. Charles Welch, librarian of the Guild-

hall, London. The earliest regulations (1348) seem
to have been drawn so as to enforce the making of a
high quality of pewter, a reputation for which has
always been the aim of " The Worshipful Company."
The original ordinances, which were drawn up and
submitted to the mayor and aldermen for their
approval, are still a part of the records, and are written
in both Latin and Norman French, according to the
ancient custom of the city. I give the first paragraph
as it runs translated by Mr. H. T. Riley, in his " Memorials of London," printed in 1868:

" First for as moche os the crafte of peuterers is founded vppon
certaine maters & metales as of brasse tyn & lede in pte of the
wheche iij metals they make vessels that is to saie pottes salers
dysshes platers and othir thinges by good folke be spoken wheche
werkes aske certaine medles & alays aftir the maner of the
uessels be spoken which thinges can not be made without goode
auisement of the peuterere experte and kunnynge in the crafte.
Therevppon the crafte goode folk of the crafte praien that it be
ordeined that iij or iiij moste trew & cunnyng of the crafte be
chosen to ouersee the alales and werkes aforesaide. And by
thaire examinacion and asay amendement to be made where the
defaute is hastely vppon the dede and if any rebel ayenst the
wardeins or assaiours than the dafaute and the name of the tres-
passour rebelle to be sent to the maire and to be iuged in the
presence of the goode folke of the Crafte that have take the defaute. And be it vnderstonde that al maner vessells of peauter
as disshes Saucers platers chargeours pottes square Cruettes
square Crismatories and othir thinges that they make square or
Cistils that they be made of fyne peauter and the mesure of
Brasse to the tyn as moche as it wol receiue of his nature of the
same and al othir thinges of the saide crafte that be wrozte as
pottes rounde that pertaine to the crafte to be wrouzte of tyn
with an aiay of lede to a resonable mesure and the mesure of
the alay of an C tyn xxvj lb. lede and that is called vessels of
tyn for euer."

The ordinance goes on to state:

That none may become a member of the craft unless he "wirke truely" and hath been an apprentice.

That none may sell pewter ware in the city till it has been assayed by the wardens and found satisfactory.

That neither is it lawful to send ware out of the city for sale, unless it has been assayed by the wardens. If such be done, he shall "be ateint afore the maire and aldermen be he punished bi theire discrecion aftir his trespasse whan he is atient at the sute of the goode folke of his crafte."

Then come the penalties to be enforced on apprentices who are dishonest, on members of the craft who do bad work, and also the rule which savours of the "closed shop,"—that none may work at night!

No man is to entice away another man's workmen, and no one is to take a workman who has not been apprenticed.

The earliest name by which this Company was known was "The Craft of Pewterers"; by 1528 it was altered to "The Craft or Mystery"; and in 1611 the words Craft and Mystery disappear, and from that date the name was "The Company of Pewterers."

Although great care is taken to give the proportions of lead and tin used in the inferior quality of pewter, which made what was known as "vessels of tin," the proportions used in "fine pewter," which is a mixture of tin and brass, is left very vague and was doubtless a trade secret.

The regulations which governed the craft were most jealously guarded and enforced, for the credit of the trade, and this was not peculiar to the pewterers alone, but common to all the guilds. By a statute passed in 1363 it was enacted that "two of every craft shall be chosen to survey that none use other craft than that same which he has chosen," which prohibited any "handy man" from getting more than his share of business.

For seventy-five years the craft prospered and grew very powerful (it was fourteenth in the list of guilds), and the Company kept taking to itself new privileges without laying the matters before the mayor and aldermen. It was brought up with a round turn by this latter body, which had no idea of seeing perquisites and power slipping from itself, and all the ordinances made previous to the year 1438, without the authority of the mayor or aldermen, were annulled.

It was further enacted that every pewterer should attend at the Pewterers' Hall when summoned, and a "bedel" was appointed to see to this matter. At the same time a table of regulations for the standard weight of vessels was drawn up, and offenders who did not make their wares conform to this standard were to be dealt with accordingly.

The different kinds of ware were made by different workmen,—plates and chargers by one set, called "Sad-ware men"; pots and vessels for liquids by another class known as "Hollow-ware men"; and spoons, little salts, and other small wares by the poorer members of the trade, who were designated "Triflers."

So great were the powers exercised by the body of pewterers that it was enabled to ask and obtain the privilege of getting a fourth part of all the tin which was brought into London, and the wardens of the craft had to see that enough tin for their use was brought from the mines of Cornwall and Devonshire, and that the merchants of the stannaries did not abuse their rights and adulterate its quality. From time to time the fact crops out that the quality of the tin sent up to London was tampered with, and there are many complaints and petitions regarding it. So many trades were affected that in 1707 the Company petitioned the Lord Treasurer with reference to the abuses in certain mines in Cornwall and Devon. The petition states that the mines produced—

—"oar of three Qualityes all verry useful . . . which qualityes render it preferrable to all other Tin in the World."

And then it goes on to relate that the—

—"constant practice & usage of the Tinners had formerly been to smelt or blow the Oar from eache mine by itselfe, at some contiguos Blowinghouse whch kept their sevrall Qualityes intire."

But it seemed that large proprietors had acquired, under Letters Patent, the right to buy from different mines and smelt down the various qualities, and thus rendering it unfit—

—"for abundance of uses wherin Tin is wholly consumed. Its quality and lustre being changed, An Scarlett Dyers, Tin ffoyl workers, Potters for all white Ware, Pinmakers, Founders, Plumbers and Glasiers . . . nor is the sd Tin of itself soe fitt to be sent to Turky and other places in Barrs nor for making fine Pewter or for Dyers Kettles &etc. And although the Pewterers of London at this time are obliged to take the Tin as it riseth or yet stand still Yet when Tin shall be free there will be a difference made in price between Tinn blown as formerly and this now complained of."

And the petition prays for some remedy of these evils.

The first record made in these books for the purchase of a number of moulds is dated 1451; they were for the use of the members, and they consisted of "plat molde, dyshe molde, Sawsyrmolde, medyl molde, Salydyshe molde, quawre molde, and Trenchor molde."

At this period (about 1450) the members of the craft seem to have been divided into two if not more classes,—the "bretheren," who took a share in the government of the craft, and the "freemen," who had to be content with the trade privileges only. "Sustren" were admitted to the craft, not only to the religious fellowship, but as working members, since the audit books show that they made their contributions, which are included in the accounts. Yet, even so, in 1590 it was ordered that—

—"whereas Andrew bowyar hath herto fore byne admonyshed for settynge a worke a woman to graue vppon his pewter contrary to the ordynaunce of the house and hath payed his fyne for it, at this court he is charged agayne for the lyke offence and now he is adiuged to paye V.s. for a fyne and yf ever he be found to do the lyke then he shall paye the vtmost of the fyne whch is iij. li."

Many functions were observed by the Company other than those of mere business. Its members always attended the funerals of those of the craft who died, and the charges for "drynke" are duly set down. Before the Company took possession of its "Greate Hall," it rented a hall of the Austin Friars, and from the Grey Friars the use of a hall for the three great religious festivals of the year,—Christmas, Easter, and the Feast of the Assumption. The altar was kept

bright at the expense of the craft, although it is noted
that some half-burned candles were returned to the
chandler who furnished them, and were duly allowed
for in his account.

Even before its incorporation, the Guild had owned
a seal, and, as its patroness was the Virgin Mary, part
of the device of the Company was two lily pots, which
appeared on either side of the Virgin's figure.

The Company also paid for the " Bedel, his gown,"
and as he was the most important paid official of the
company it was a good one. He lived at the Hall,
and went with the masters and wardens when they
were on searches for pewter which was not up to the
standard, and sometimes he went on searches by himself. Besides hunting down delinquent pewterers he
kept the Hall in order, summoned all the " bretheren "
to the meetings, paid the alms, and, under the charge
of the master and wardens, superintended the purchase
of tin, lead, etc., saw to the renting of moulds, stamping of wares, and, in fact, kept up all the trade relations
of the Company.

The guilds of London were great and important
bodies, bound by their charters to render many duties
to the city. They were called upon to defend it, as
well as to act in concert with the governor of the
Tower and furnish men for its defence in times of war
or civil commotion. There are numerous entries for
such service in the interesting records of the Pewterers'
Company, and one of the first of these is in 1460, when
the Company furnished two men fully armed, whom
they maintained at London Bridge for thirty days.

The history of these great guilds is really English history, and in the pages of their records we see reflected the struggles and turmoils which were agitating England. About this same time (1463) Edward IV was coming from Sheen to London by water, and the citizens of London, who had given him great assistance, went joyfully forth to meet him, and all the guilds and corporations combined to give him a fitting and stately welcome. The Pewterers' Guild was not behind the other and more powerful guilds, hiring a boat and a barge, " for to goo wt the kyng to resceiue hym atte his comyng."

The companies gave their attendance to the mayor seven times a year when he went to church, or, as it is recorded, " to Paules,"—St. Paul's being the church where services were held with the greatest state. These seven occasions were Allhallow's Day (November 1), Christmas Day, St. Stephen's Day (December 26), St. John's Day (December 27), New Year's Day, Twelfth Day, and Candlemas Day. They also attended the mayor when he went to take the oath of office at Westminster on St. Simon's and St. Jude's Day (October 28), and the wardens of the Pewterers' Guild had a place at the mayor's feast, being fourteenth in the order of precedence, and being represented by five persons besides the wardens. Those who were not invited to the Guildhall, where the dinner was held, had a dinner provided for them elsewhere at the cost of the stewards.

On January 20, 1473, Edward IV gave a charter to the Company, by which it became a corporation.

This charter greatly enlarged its powers and extended its control over all England. By this means its searches for inferior ware were carried on throughout the whole country, and much "ley-metal," or under-quality pewter, was brought to London, where it was bought by the wardens and used again with sufficient good metal added to bring it up to the requirements.

That there was need for these frequent searches, the following item, taken from that valuable repository of manners and customs, "The Paston Letters," goes to show. Madam Paston, writing from Norwich, England, in 1452, to her husband in London, says:

"Right worshipful husband, I commend me to you. I pray you that ye will buy two dozen trenchers, for I can get none fit in this town."

In 1461 the same conditions apparently still exist, for he is in London as before, and she writes him:

"Alsoe if ye be at home this Christmas it were well done ye should purvey a garnish or train of pewter vessels, two basins, two ewers, and twelve candlesticks for ye have too few of any of these to serve this place."

Although this lady seems very subservient and meek to her husband, she was a terror to her family. One of the family friends was a certain Stephen Scrope, and to show how lax were the ideas of the times, I quote a line from one of his letters: "For very need I was fain to sell a little daughter I have for much less than I should." In after years, when this same Scrope was quite an old man, he wished to marry Madam Paston's young daughter, and the girl was quite willing to take him provided he could show that his land was not burdened with debt. Her readiness does not seem so singular when we read that the poor girl was kept in confinement by her mother, who beat her at least twice a week, so that she writes to her brother, "My head is continually broken in two or three places!" She also says that if the Scrope marriage cannot be arranged she hopes he will hurry and find some one else for her. It is pleasant to know that she did find somebody, and seems to have been reasonably happy.

Madam Paston was by no means a person of low degree, but the whole thing is typical of the low and material view of life which prevailed during the period of the Wars of the Roses, and indeed for many years after. It is well-nigh impossible to conceive how at this time the barest necessaries were limited. The daily bath was a thing unknown, for, though centuries before, in the southern countries, the elegance and convenience of the splendid baths, where both hot and cold water were supplied, were notorious, the abuses engendered by them had brought about their suppression. Soap-balls and cleansing-balls were in use, to be sure, but they rather glossed over than remedied evils. The houses were kept in a condition which can only be guessed at, since such morsels as were not eaten at table were thrown among the rushes with which the floor was strewed, and were shared with the dogs, whose leavings were in turn devoured by rats and mice. Often these rushes remained on the floor for a week at a time, or perhaps more, and when they grew too dusty they were sprinkled. One may guess why "essences and flower-waters" were chosen for this sprinkling.

The rich prelates, whose furred and silken garments were the mates to those of royalty itself, did not allow their tables to be any less richly spread. They owned pewter very early, for when John Ely, vicar of Ripon, died in 1427, he left, among other things, "di.dus. garnes de vessel de pewdre cum ij chargiours."

The College of Auckland had in its storerooms in 1498, "xx pewder platters, xij pewder dyshes, viii salters, ii paire of potclyppes, j garnishe of vessel, j shaving basyn."

In the Convent of the Holy Cross, at Erfurt, Saxony, as far back as 1470, there were found one hundred and fifty pewter amphoræ, seventy cups, jugs, porringers, etc., and at St. Cyr, two hundred pewter amphoræ, with a number of flagons and tankards.

In 1575 the Archbishop of Canterbury possessed—

—"eighteen score and ten pounds of pewter vessels in the kitchen, in jugs, basins, porringers, sauce-boats, pots, and nineteen candlesticks; also pewter measures in the wine cellar, eight pewter salts in the pantry at Lambeth, and two garnishes of pewter with spoons, at Croyden."

The demand for pewter vessels, which had crowded out wooden utensils and those of horn, continued, and it was as early as 1474 that the marking of pewter is first noted. All inferior pewter was to be stamped with a "broad arrow," which showed that it was to be forfeited, and then consigned to the melting-pot and recast with new metal.

The "touch-mark," which is so often spoken of in connection with pewter, is the mark of the maker of each particular piece, and it may be his name, or his name accompanied by some device, like a rose, a figure, or an animal. At first no list of these marks was kept by the Company, nor was there any registration fee. There are, however, at the Pewterers' Hall in London, five great boards on which many marks are stamped. The earliest marks are very small, and were initials only, so that it is impossible to identify many of them, though the marks on these plates went back as far as the middle of the fifteenth century.

There is a record in the books, in the year 1492, of a charge of two shillings for "markyn Irons for hollow ware men," and this must have been for official use by the Company, though what the device was, is not known.

In 1503 there was made the first compulsory enactment for the affixing of the name of the maker upon all articles of pewter, though the practice had been in use for years without compulsion. If a pewterer declined to mark his ware he was fined five shillings or more, probably according to the will of the master. The great fairs which were held in various parts of England, like the fair at St. Albans or at Stourbridge, were also "searched" for illegal pewter, and in 1558, at both these places, fines were levied. At "Saynt albones" was "taken of George bate of alesbury a sawcr." The second fining is more curious still, for at "sturbridge fayer of harry Ratclyf was taken a platter not marked, and he marched in company wth a french woman."

There are given many inventories, taken from time to time, of the contents of the Company's Hall and of all their property. These are extremely interesting, but very long, and in every one is mentioned, "A Table of Pewter wt euery man's marke therein."

As early as 1552 it was customary to make pewter covers for the coarse stone pots which were used as drinking-vessels. In order that these lids should come up to the standard, it was ordered that—

—"all those that lyd stone pottes should set their own marke on the in syde of the lyd & to bring in all such stone pottes in to the hall wherby they maye be vewed yf they be workmanly wrought & so be markyd wt the marck of the hall on the owt syde of the Lyd. Also euery one that makyth such stone pottes shall make anew marck such one as the mr and wardens shalbe pleasid wtall whereby they maye be known from this daye forward. Theise pottes to be brought in wekly vpon the satterdaye and yf the satterdaye be holly daye then to bring them in vpon the ffrydaye. And loke who dotd the contrary shall forfayte for euery stone pott so duely provyd iiij d. in mony over and beseyde the forfayte of all such pottes as be not brought in according to this artycle."

The payment for marking these pots was small, for apparently some were brought to the Hall for marking.

"At the same Courte the mr Wardens and assystants wth the hole clothing hath graunted that John Curtys shoulde haue ffor markyng of every dosyn of stone pottes whosesoever brought them to marck one ffarthing."

The rules for the marking of wares were constantly before the Company, and many were the fines imposed. By 1564 the rose and crown had become so important a mark that the following regulation concerning its use was framed:

"Also it is agreed that euery one of the saide felowship that makith any warre shall set his owne marke theron. And that no man shall geue for his proper marck or touch the Rose and crown wt lettrs nor otherwise but only to whome it is geuen by the felowship. Nor that no man of the saide craft shall geue one anothers marck nother wt lettrs nor otherwise, but euery one to geue a sondry marck such one as shalbe alowed by the maister and wardens for the tyme beinge vpon payne to forfaite and paye for euery tyme offendinge to the Crafte's boxe xiij s. iiij d."

In the year 1592 it was ordered by the court—

—"that all the company shall set ther tuches vppon a new plat and that they shall paye ii.d. a pece and one penny to the clarke ane one to the bedel."

Pewter was by this time pretty generally distributed over the kingdom, and where, a century before, it had been owned chiefly by the rich, now it appears in the wills of the middle classes. James Flynt, Jr., died in 1561, at "ye piche of Matloke" (Derbyshire). Among other things he leaves—

—"to sonne & heyre harry my gretest brasse pott, a greit arke, a greit satt & Ironspytt, and a greit Dubler of Pewtr & Iron Crowe and a mattocke."

At the end of the sixteenth century Harrison wrote:

"Such furniture of household of this mettall, as we commonly call by the name of vessell, is sold usually by the garnish which doth containe 12 platters, 12 dishes, 12 saucers and these are either of silver fashion, or else with brode or narrow brims and bought by the pound, which is now valued at sevenpence or peradventure at eightpence."

The court took into its hands many other things

besides the business affairs of the members. Of course this was true of the other guilds as well. For instance, it was set down—

—"tuchyng how that all howsholders shall governe ther servauntes and howshold accordyng vnto the precept sent fro my L maier dated the XXII of Apryll."

In order to keep the business still further in their own hands, and suppress the sale of pewter by hawkers, the whole company promised at this court, under a penalty of five pounds for default, that they would serve "no ware to any man who they knowe to be hawkers or mayntayners of hawkers."

In 1602 the Company chose to make an example of a certain "John frethene," who, being only a journeyman, still bought and sold as a householder, even though he did not give his touch to the Company or ask leave to open a shop. For these offences the court fined him seventeen shillings on four counts, and took his note that he would pay the fines before Candlemas.

By 1663 there were so many pewterers both in and out of London that it became necessary to keep a sharp lookout on the touch-marks, and the "Genll Court" ordered "that all tuches bee made wth the date 63 and yt they bee registered in a boke at ye hall wthin a month." This book has been lost, so that unfortunately the only touch-marks are those which are to be found on the five touch-plates which still remain to the Company.

The Company, under the supervision of the master and wardens, continued to exercise the greatest care

that the wares which were made by its members should
be of standard quality. Severe penalties were laid
on any erring brother who was discovered: he was
not only fined, but imprisoned, brought before the
Company, and made to confess his fault and to pray
for leniency that he might become a member once
more, and to bring in and yield up his old touch, and
" haue for his tuch a duble ff," which meant false
ware. Besides all these penalties already mentioned,
he had also to give up all the wares which he had
already made and which were in his shop.

The Company not only seized the false ware made
in England, but it also exercised control over all that
was sold,—in London at least. In 1656 the court
ordered that all the ware seized should be melted
" downe and Sould for Lay except the frenchmans
ware and ye dutch ware and Marsh ware." Although
the maker of inferior ware was always obliged to
change his " tuch," the terrible " ff " was not always
the punishment. Sometimes a knot was ordered to
be added to the old touch, and sometimes the offender
had to take an entirely new device. On other occasions the fraudulent makers were obliged to add the
year to their touch-mark, so that it " maie be knowne
whoe were the offenders therein."

No member of the Company was allowed to have
more than one mark at a time; and if the mark was too
large to be conveniently put on small pieces, then the
pewterer was allowed to have a smaller copy of his
great mark made, but he had to leave the impressions
of both marks with the Company. When a man

bought out the business of another, by the permission of the court he was allowed to use the first man's touch, provided he had his permission also. At one time the members of the Company got into trouble by stamping their ware with the mark of the Goldsmiths' Company, and rules were duly framed to meet this need.

We often hear the term "silver pewter," used no doubt with a view to enhancing the value of the object, but it is hardly likely that a metal like tin should be mixed with silver. Of itself, tin is extremely brittle, and to add silver enough to give it any value would be but to increase this quality. Sebaldus Ruprecht, working in the fourteenth century, made himself and his wares famous, because they so closely resembled silver, while another German, Melchior Koch, had a process by which he made his pewter look like pure gold. Such workers as these caused the Goldsmiths' Company to become uneasy, and in 1579 they secured an enactment that no pewterer should work in any metal but pewter, binding themselves at the same time not to work in that metal themselves. They had made a similar regulation in Paris as early as 1545, and in Nuremberg in 1579, the same year as in England.

A Major Purling invented in 1652 an alloy which he called "Silvorum," but the Pewterers' Company would have none of it, and would not consent to allow one of their members to work with its inventor. The Company also prohibited Lawrence Dyer from selling "untouch ware, and making of false plat called Silvorum, the which ware is ceased and detayned by the Company."

The order not to use the word "London" on the touch of any maker was issued in 1676. This was modified by 1690, and it was agreed that a member might add the word "London" to his touch in addition to the rose and crown, and to the letter "X," denoting extraordinary ware.

Country pewterers had the bad habit of adding the word "London" to the stamp of their own name, and as their wares often did not come up to the standard demanded by the Company there were many complaints. Although this practice gave the Company much trouble, and came before it from time to time for a hundred years, the matter was finally dropped in 1740, when a committee which had been appointed to investigate reported that nothing could be done to prevent country pewterers from striking "London" or "Made in London" on their ware, without application to Parliament.

Just about this time a protest was sent over from Philadelphia that the "Guinea Basons" sent from the city of Bristol to America were of inferior quality, and some redress was demanded.

Another source of trouble to the pewterers came from the "Crooked Lane" men, the name of whose place of business was indicative of their methods. Whether in some underhand way they imported vessels of inferior metal, or whether they themselves made some kind of tin ware, is not now known; but that they were a serious annoyance to the craft is evident from the fact that £50 (a large sum in 1634) was paid for the—

—"suppressing of the excesse and abusive making of Crooked Lane ware, whereby the so doing and counterfeiting of the reall commodity of Tynn is to the greate deceit or wrong of his Ma'ties subjects."

Although the Crooked Lane men tried to get a charter for their goods in 1669, nothing seems to have come of it.

While it was obligatory that each maker should place his name on his ware, it was not necessary that he should put on the rose and crown. In some cases certain articles were stamped with certain marks; as, for instance, the pewter lids of drinking-pots, which it was ordered should have on them a *fleur-de-lys*. This rule had been in order since 1548.

There were very definite regulations as to what the standard weight of pewter vessels should be. I give the " new table," which was made April 14, 1673, since it most nearly approximates the time which would be of peculiar interest to us in America.

DISHES, 15 sizes from 20 lb. to one half pound weight, weights as implied in their description, *i.e.,* a 20 lb. dish to weigh 20 lb., and so on.

PLATES, $1\frac{1}{4}$ lb., each dozen $15\frac{1}{2}$ lb.; 1 lb., each dozen 13 lb.; $\frac{3}{4}$ lb., each dozen 10 lb.

GUINIE BASONS, 6 sizes from 4 lb. to 1 lb. weights as described.

BEDD PANNS, great $4\frac{1}{2}$ lb., middle $3\frac{1}{2}$ lb., small 3 lb.

LAVERS, great 5 lb., middle 4 lb., small 3 lb.

FLAGGONS, great pottle 8 lb., small pottle 6 lb., three pint 4 lb., quart 3 lb.

EFRAM and other Potts, three quart $4\frac{1}{2}$ lb., two quart 3 lb. 2 oz., three pint 2 lb. 2 oz., quart 1 lb. 10 oz., pint 1 lb. 2 oz., half pint $\frac{3}{4}$ lb.

WINCHESTER QUART, each shall weigh $1\frac{1}{4}$ lb.

GUINEY POTTS OR TUNN PINTES, each dozen 12 lb.

LONG AND SHORT CANN, each $\frac{3}{4}$ lb.

NEW FASHIONED TANKARDS, great quart $2\frac{1}{4}$ lb., small quart 2 lb., four inches $1\frac{3}{4}$ lb., pint $1\frac{1}{2}$ lb., ordinary four inches 1 lb. 6 oz.

STOOLE PANS, 5 lb. 4 lb. 3 lb. $2\frac{1}{2}$ lb. of same weight.

FRENCH AND SQUARE CANDLESTICKS, great, middle, small, smallest, $5\frac{1}{2}$ ib., $4\frac{1}{2}$ lb., $3\frac{1}{2}$ lb., $2\frac{1}{2}$ lb., each pair.

FLAT CANDLESTICKS, great, middle, round, smallest, $4\frac{1}{2}$ lb., $3\frac{1}{2}$ lb., $2\frac{1}{4}$ lb., $1\frac{3}{4}$ lb., each pair.

BELL CANDLESTICKS, 1 lb., $\frac{3}{4}$ lb. to weigh $2\frac{1}{4}$ lb., $1\frac{1}{2}$ lb. each pair.

PORRENGERS.

Great pints, each dozen 9 lb.; small pints each dozen $7\frac{1}{2}$ lb.

Bosse, six sizes varying in weight each dozen from 7 lb. to 2 lb.

Ordinary blood porrengers, each dozen $1\frac{1}{2}$ lb.

Guinney, each dozen $3\frac{1}{2}$ lb.

Great corded, middle, small, each dozen respectively 9 lb., 8 lb., $6\frac{1}{4}$ lb.

SAWCERS.

Slight, great per gross 22 lb., small per gross 14 lb.

New fashioned swaged; great, middle, small, each dozen respectively 7 lb., 5 lb., 4 lb.

LAY.

Wine measures; gallon 10 lb., pottle 6 lb., quart 3 lb., pint 2 lb., half pint 1 lb., quarter pint 8 lb. each dozen, half quarter pint 4 lb. each dozen.

STILL HEADS, being 9, 10, 11, 12, inches at bottom to weigh 9, 10, 11, 12 lb., 13 inches 15 lb., 14 inches 17 lb.

AND it is by this Court further Ordered that the weight of STANDISHES shall be as followeth (vist):

GREAT water large with Lyons $2\frac{1}{2}$ lb., great Water plaine 2 lb., middle Water wth Lyons 2 lb., middle water plaine 1 lb. 10 oz., Small water wth Lyons $1\frac{3}{4}$ lb., Small water plaine 1 lb. 6 oz., Long Till with Lyons 1 lb. 6 oz., Long Till plaine 1 lb., Round Water wth Lyons 1 lb., Round Water plaine $\frac{3}{4}$ lb.

Merchants who sold these vessels were to charge four-pence more than cost price, and transportation, except for some special objects like "guinney basons."

Admission to the Company of Pewterers and permission to follow the trade was by no means the simple thing it seems. There were only two ways by which a would-be pewterer could gain a foothold in the body,—by serving his time as an apprentice with a member of the craft, or by patrimony. In 1688 two men applied for the freedom of the Company and were denied, although one of them had a brother who was a member, and the other conducted the business for a relative whose death had left it in his hands. This latter man, a merchant tailor by trade, though he had gained " competent skill " in the trade of pewterer, was not allowed to become a trader " upon any terms whatsoever." At this same time one Geffers, a " Free pewterer of Corke who had fled thence from danger of his life through persecution, prayed Leave to work or be releived." The Company would not allow him to work, but granted him twenty shillings in relief. Another case was that of a French pewterer who had suffered so much for his religion that he had barely escaped from France with his life and had lost all his property. He prayed to be allowed to continue his work, but was permitted only to do so " privately in his own chamber," and that but for the space of a few months.

The practice of putting the address of one's shop or place of business on the ware was much frowned upon at first, and it was not allowed to be placed on the ware at all. Indeed you might not even extol the quality of your own ware, and in 1590 there appears this entry in the books: " A fyne of Richard Staple ffor boastyng his wares to be better than the other mens, iij s. iiij d." Nor was it allowed to disperse "tickets," with name and abode on them, about the city, and in 1690 one Robert Lock was reprimanded for so doing, but denied the charge.

By the eighteenth century the members of the Company were divided into three classes: the Livery or Clothing men,—" brotheren that paien quarterege "; the Yeomanry or Freemen, that were not " brotheren," but paid quarterage all the same; and the Covenant men or Apprentices, who served the second class, who were their masters. The lot of the apprentices was by no means one of ease, for they were liable to be punished by being put in the stocks or kept in the pillory all the market time. They were not allowed to be absent from work, nor to take part " at any unlawful game as dising bowling and Carding." If they did, and were caught, they were brought before the Lord Mayor, who could mete out such punishment as he deemed proper. They were obliged to attend church with their masters, and to have their hair cut, not being allowed to " weare unseemly haire not befitting an apprentice "; and in 1572 a proclamation was issued "tendinge to the reformacion of the greate abuse latelie practized by Apprentizes in excesse of apparraile." This was some of the rulings of " Good Queen Bess," who would not allow the wearing of "ye Ruffes " by her subjects except in such widths as she deemed proper. Her own ruffs, of finest lawn and lace, stiffened with " devil's broth," as starch was called, and held out with underproppers of wire, were as extravagant as fancy could devise. They swelled with the "proper arch of pride," and encircled her auburn head like a halo, but all city folk, even the clergy, had to conform to the width of ruff she deemed proper for them, and such as offended were likely to have the objectionable ruff measured by the guard and its superfluity lopped off.

The apprentices were punished for purchasing metal privately, for refusing to work for former masters, for making any articles "free," and they were not permitted to receive wages. They were also expected to serve as "whifflers" at pageants and processions,— that is, they had to run ahead and keep the way clear; and they served at banquets; so, as may be seen, their position was hardly enviable.

The members of the craft brought into the treasury generous sums from the renting of their pewter plate. A "garnish" was a small supply,—a dozen each of platters, plates, and small plates; and there were not many households which owned more, so "feast vessels" were often rented. The members became too free in borrowing the Company plate, for in 1656 this rule was laid down:

"It is ordered that the pewter of the Hall shall not bee lent to any of the Membrs of this Company or to any but vpon Spetial occasion for his or there pticular vses as in case of wedding or other grand occasion of their one, nor then neither wthout Spetill lisence of the Mastr and wardens first had been obtayned."

No new pewter was rented out, but only that which had been in use. Even royalty was not above renting it in their need, and all the city companies owned more or less, which they were as ready to rent as the Pewterers themselves. At Queen Anne's coronation feast much pewter was used, and the tale has come down that quantities of it were stolen.

From time to time we find records of large stocks of private pewter, and some of them very early too. Edward I had more than three hundred pieces in his own use. The Universities of Cambridge and Oxford had services and cups of pewter as early as 1470, but it is nearly all gone now, silver plate having taken its place.

Drinking-vessels, whether in the form of beakers, mugs, tankards, or earthen pots with lids of pewter, early formed an important part of the pewterers' trade. Harrison, in his "Description of England," says:

"As for drinke it is usuallie filled in pots, gobblets, jugs, bols of silver in noblemens houses, also in fine Venice glasses of all formes, and for want of these, elsewhere, in pots of earth of sundrie colours and moulds, whereof manie are garnished with silver, or at the leastwise in pewter."

The Pewterers' Company wished to control the trade with regard to taverns, and the weight of pots, pottle pots, and tankards was definitely decided upon. To show that the Company had more than the silversmiths to contend with, I quote from Heywood's "Philocothonista," published in 1635, in which he speaks of the cups then in use:

"Of drinking cups divers and sundry sorts we have; some of elme, some of box, some of maple, some of holly, etc., maziers, broad-mouthed dishes, noggins, whiskins, piggins, crinzes, ale-bowls, wassell-bowls, court-dishes, tankards, cannes, from a pottle to a pint, from a pint to a gill. Other bottles we have of leather, but they are most used among the shepherds and harvest people of the country. Small Jacks we have in many of the ale-houses of the cities and suburbs, tipt with silver, besides the great black jacks and bombards at the court, which when the Frenchmen first saw they reported at their return into their own country, that the Englishmen used to drink out of their bootes. We have besides cups made of the hornes of beasts, of the eggs of ostriches, others made of the shells of divers fishes brought from the Indes and other places, and shining like mother of pearl. Come to plate, every taverne can afford you flat bowles, French bowles, prounet bowles, beare bowels, beakers; and private house-holders in the citie when they make a feast to entertaine their friends can furnish their cupboards with flagons, tankards, biere-cups, wine-bowles, some white, some parcell gilt, some gilt all over, some with covers, others without of sundry shapes and sizes."

Although our author does not mention pewter in all this list, it is very certain that most of the tavern ware was of this useful metal. The weight of a pottle pot, which was one that held two quarts, was to be seven and a half pounds, and the others in proportion. Perhaps no articles made by the Company were so rigorously made to conform to the standard as these same tavern measures, and severe fines were inflicted when its members offended, as may be seen from the following regulation:

"Also it is agreed that none of the felowship shall make any tankerd quarte nor tankerd pinte nor sell of those kynd of potte for any mony or otherwise but only the therdendale and half therdendale accordinge to the Lawes and constitucion of this Citie. And also the pot called the brode pynt And that no holowaremen shall make any potte of Just quarte or pynte for ale and beare measure but only the stope pottell the great stope quart and the great stope pynt, and the great pynt with the Brode Bottam the greate English pottell the greate English quarte and the great English pynt and none other. And as for taverne ware to make them according to the assice and as by example remaynyng in owre hall And who so euer offendeth to the contrary and true meanyng hereof shalbe comitted to the warde there to remayne vntil he haue paide xl s. for euery tyme offending the one moitie of which forfaiture to be to the Chaumbrlayne of london and the other moitie to the Crafte boxe."

In the latter part of the sixteenth century it was found that measures were being made which did not conform to the standard agreed upon, and the man who made them was thereupon disciplined, as it was ordered—

—" that from hence furthe, Roger Hawkesforde, shall not make any moe wyne pottes, wherebie to sell or vtter the same, of that molde or fasshion, nowe at this presente daie, shewed, before the maister, Wardeins, and assistaunces, for that by there greate breadthe in the mouthe and shortness, throughoute, there appearethe, a manifeste deceite in measure, to all other the queenes maiesties, subiectes, receyvinge wyne, by suche their saide curtalled, and uniuste measure."

In the next year (1575) an offender was still more severely dealt with, as he made pots of ley metal. On account of his humble subjection he was excused this time, but warned that on the second offence he should be expelled from the Company for ever, and, as it was, he was obliged to give up his touch and was given a new one.

There were constant alterations in the making of tavern ware, and by 1638 there were so many different kinds in use that the Pewterers' Company drew up a petition to the king concerning the matter.

Fig. 19.   PEWTER GROUP
3, 4, 5, *Tea Service Formerly Belonging to Sir Walter Scott.*
6, 7, *Tumblers*
8, 9, *Toddy and Soup Ladles*

"Certaine Articles or propositions were read [December 12, 1638] wch are desired to be propounded to his Matie, and ye same by his Gracious pleasure to be graunted. The whch were all well liked by the Genll Comp.

1st. That ye Measures for Beare, Ale, Milke, and ye like be of pewter and sealed according to a statute in ye case prouided.

2d. That noe Candlesticks, Pye Plates, Pie Coffins, chamber potts, Pastie platts, potts, or other dishes be made of white plate whch doth hinder ye consumption of Tynne.

3d. That all forragn Ware, from ffrance, Holland, etc., be prohibited.

4th. That ye Comp. of Pewterers of London may have power and Authoretie to search and sease all falce mettal and wares in Ireland and Scotland, according as in England is Prouided by Statute."

The "pie coffins" referred to were moulds in which pies were baked, and the "white metal" which they desired suppressed was silver. All the time new vessels were coming into use, and the struggles which the pewterers made to keep their wares well to the front were unceasing. The use and sale of liquor was growing more and more, and at last the Company informed the Court that "there was a great increase of Muggs made of Earth and a Mark impressed thereon in imitacon of Sealed Measures to sell liquid Comodities in." This was about 1702, when the pottery Bellarmines were beginning to be freely made, and the Elers Brothers were potting too, and ware was being brought into England by every ship which came from the Orient.

There were also what were called "knot bowls," and "mazer bowls," these latter being drinking-bowls made from maple-wood (the old name of maple being "mazer"), and these were bound or tipped with silver or pewter, and indeed were frequently lined with these metals. I know of one such bowl, bound with silver and standing on delicate little legs, which was the property of a wealthy Dutch *fvrow* in Schenectady in 1736. It has come down through various members of the family, together with some of her silver, and makes a much-treasured heirloom.

At an auction sale in London in 1905 one of these mazer bowls, which dated from the seventeenth century, was sold for several thousand dollars, many collectors being anxious to secure it.

Besides the mugs which are so constantly spoken of, there were beakers and tankards. The former was a drinking-vessel generally without handles, small at the bottom, and sloping outward at the top. These are found in inventories at the very beginning of the seventeenth century. In England at the present day one will be more likely to find them in the collector's cabinet than among the heirlooms of great people or even among the treasures of corporations. These are the beakers of English make, for it is much easier to find those of Dutch origin or from the countries of northern Europe.

Dr. Johnson suggests that the origin of the name was "beak," and defined the "beaker" as "a cup with a spout in the form of a bird's beak." Other authorities say that it was a kind of vessel derived from Flanders or Germany, without fixing its shape; and Forby claims to trace it to the Saxon "bece" (beech),—"ordinary drinking-vessels being made of beech-wood." De Laborde gets the English word "byker" from the French word *bukct,* giving as his authorities the cases where the latter is used to mean a holy-water bucket or a large cup with a cover.

In Scotland the beaker seemed to be a favourite form of communion-cup in the seventeenth century. Some early references are as follows:

1346.—"ciphum meum biker argenti."—From the will of a canon of York.

1348.—"Bikers, cups intended for ladies."—Memorials of the Order of the Garter, by Beltz.

1399.—"Two bikers of silver gilt, 29 oz., one other biker gilt, 16 oz.—From the list of a jeweller's stock in Cheapside.

1625.—"One white beaker."—From the inventory of Edward Waring of Lea, Esq."

These references are to utensils of silver, but beakers were made of pewter as well, and in some cases it was sought to conceal the nature of the metal with paint. In 1622 a search was conducted at Lambeth Marsh, where were found " divers peece of painted pewter " of bad workmanship. They were taken from two "aliens," John Heath and Anthony Longsay, and the pieces are referred to in the following manner:

"1 great Bealer pte white marked wth the Starre. Starton."
"Afterwards in Bedlam, in the house of Paull Dickenson, Heath and Longsays ptner weare some smallest paynted beakers and salts."

Tankards, on the contrary, were large at the base and sloped up to a smaller mouth, and had handles and lids. This was the commonest type, but there were also tankards with straight sides and with bowl-shaped bodies. On the handles of many tankards are to be found whistles. These date from Jacobean times, and were used to summon the drawer when " fresh drinks all round " were wanted by the company. Little by little the whistles fell into disuse, but the tankard-makers kept on in their old fashion and made the handles of just the same shape. There were also " puzzle " handles for the confusion of a green customer. If he failed to put his finger over a hole, the liquor either failed to come out, or spilled over, or did some other unexpected thing which tended to his confusion and to the mirth of the company, which was always alive to all species of horse-play and considered the stranger fair game.

Before the days of individual cups of all kinds it was the custom to pass among the company the cup which cheered as well as inebriated, and there was difficulty in so arranging that each guest should have his due share and no more. This was finally obviated by having, in the inside of the cup, pegs or marks upon the side, so that each drinker could tell how much was his portion, and the company looked to it that each one drank fair. The correctness of the use of the word " tankard " as referring to a drinking-vessel is seldom questioned, but Mr. Cripps, in his interesting volume on " Old English Plate," snows a different origin.

" The use of the word ' tankard ' in its now familiar sense of a large drinking-vessel with a cover and a handle is of comparatively modern introduction. No article of plate is called by that name in any of the volumes of wills and inventories published by the Surtees Society, which carry us to the year 1600 The word seems to first occur in this sense about 1575, and from

Fig. 20. ENGLISH PEWTER
Collection of Mrs. Charles Barry

that time is constantly applied to the vessels that have been ever since known as tankards.[1]

"In earlier days it was used for the wooden tubs bound with iron, and containing some three gallons, in which water was carried. The men who fetched the water from the conduits in London were called 'tankard bearers,' and in a Coroner's Roll of 1276, for the ward of Castle Bayard, tankards are mentioned as the vessels they bore. This roll sets forth that one Greene, a water-carrier, who had come to St. Paul's Wharf, 'cu quodam tancardo,' intending to take up water with it, entered a boat there, and, after filling the tankard, attempted to place it on the wharf, but the weight of the water in the tankard making the boat move away as he was standing on its board, he fell into the water between the boat and the wharf, and was drowned, as the coroner found, by misadventure.

"Again, in 1337, the keepers of the conduits received a sum of money for rents 'for tynes and tankards,' thereat; and in 1350 a house is hired for one year at 10s. to put the tankards in,—les tanquers,—and two irons were bought for stamping them.

"Similar utensils are found in farming accounts of the same period. In 1294 at Framlingham, Suffolk Co., the binding with iron of thirteen tankards cost 3s., and six years later a three-gallon iron-bound tankard is priced in Cambridge at 1s. At Leatherhead a two-gallon tankard is valued at 2d. in 1338, and two such vessels at Eltham together cost 4d. in 1364."

Yet even in the sixteenth century the word "tankard" was not exclusively applied to a drinking-vessel, for in 1567, in a church account, I find a notice of "lether" tankards, which had nothing to do with drinking-cups, for these objects were used as fire-buckets. There is still another application of the word to be found in a churchwarden's inventory of about the same period (1566), in which he mentions "a penny

[1] Mr. Cripps is hardly correct here, for "tankard pots" were frequently mentioned in the Pewterers' Company's records as early as 1480, nearly one hundred years before the time given by him.

tanckard of wood used as a holy-water stock." Sometimes, even in the seventeenth century, tankards appear in the inventories of household goods among the kitchen utensils, as "two tankards and one payle," and this was as late as 1625.

However, the transference of the word used to express a water-tub, to a small vessel for holding liquid, does not seem at all out of the way, and is so entirely natural that the work of many learned doctors in tracing the word from other derivations appears most far-fetched. For example:

"Duchat and Thomas would bothe derive 'tankard' from 'tin-quart,' and Dr. Thomas Henshaw from the twang or sound the lid makes on shutting it down; but after all, if tank is derived, as it surely is, from the French *estang,* a pond or pool, it is not necessary to go further for a derivation of the name of a vessel which was originally intended to hold water, than to connect it with tank, and derive it from the same source."

Johnson's Dictionary describes a tankard as "a large vessel for strong drink," and cites Ben Jonson: " Hath his tankard touched your brain?"

Another form of drinking-vessel which I have frequently found in this country is called a "noggin," and is often in pewter; indeed, I have never found it in any other metal. It holds a gill, and quite a number of them may be seen in the large group depicted in Figure 19. They look something like egg-cups. The word "noggin" is an old one, and is said to be derived from the Irish word *noigen,* or the Gaelic *noigean,* and the cup has long been in use among the peasantry in the English country districts. There are some of these noggins at the Essex Institute, Salem, Mass., where, among a large collection of pewter, there are some interesting specimens. Before leaving the group in Figure 19, which has some pieces of early Britannia ware as well as pewter, notably the tea-set which belonged to Sir Walter Scott, I would call attention to the different tankards, many of them of an early type.

Among other drinking-cups of some centuries ago were what we should call "loving-cups," but which were really caudle-cups, posset-cups, or posnets. They had two handles, were often provided with covers, and sometimes stood on trays or stands. They were somewhat pear-shaped, swelling into larger bowls at the base, and were used for drinking posset, which was milk curdled with wine and other additions. The curd floated above the liquor, and, rising into the narrow part of the cup, could be easily removed, leaving the clear fluid at the bottom. Their fashion differs slightly with their date. A fine specimen is shown in Figure 20. It is a solid piece, and is marked on the outside with a crown, a star, and the word "quart." The dish with handles beside it is marked "Made in London" and "Hard metal," though there is no maker's mark on it. The decoration is very crude, a sort of wriggled work, showing a boar's head in a shield. These handles are movable, and are very different from the ears, or stiff handles, which were common on dishes and bowls at this time.

In Figure 21 are depicted what we in America are apt to call porringers, though in England they are variously known as ear-dishes, bowls, bleeding-dishes, or posnets, as well as porringers. They are of extremely ancient make, and in an inventory dated 1537 they are spoken of as "counterfettes or podingers," "iij counterfettes therwise called podingers of pewter, whearof on is olde." These little bowls are strongly made, generally have large ears or handles of punched work, and are said to be of Dutch origin. However, many of them were made in England of varying sizes, and there were rules and regulations in abundance with regard to their manufacture. It was particularly forbidden to solder on the ears, but this rule was evaded and at length disused, so that we often find these bowls without one or both ears, the solder having been melted out or given way to use.

Bleeding-dishes were often made in nests, and were marked on the inside with rings, so that the "chicurgeon" could tell how much blood he was letting. Those of the early years of the eighteenth century measure about four and a half inches across; they have but one handle, and are by no means uncommon. The graduated rings on the inside always proclaim their use. When the bowl has but one handle and no rings on its interior, it is called a taster, and reference to these utensils may be constantly found in inventories from the time of Queen Elizabeth down. Rarely more than one is mentioned in the belongings of one person, and possibly they were originally used when poisoning was not uncommon, and the "taster" was an official in every royal household.

Fig. 21. VARIOUS TYPES OF BOWLS. ENGLISH

In the inventory of Dr. Perne, Master of Peter-house, Cambridge, England, dated 1589, there are the following items:

"Item, a white taster xiij ouncs,
Item, a white taster with a cover, xiiij ouncs."

"White metal" was silver, but tasters were more common in the baser metal.

A silver bowl called "le taster" is mentioned in a Bristol will of 1403, and in another of 1545 occurs a "taster of silver waing by estymacion vi ounces." Half-way between these two dates is a "taster with a cover," included in an inventory of 1487 attached to the will of Robert Morton, Gent, in the third year of Henry VII's reign. One of these tasters with a singularly handsome handle is shown in Figure 22. You will observe that it is slightly smaller at the top, which is made firmer by a moulded ring. The large dishes in this picture are chargers, and are quite similar to the style of dishes which were used as alms-dishes both in this country and in Great Britain. The ladle seems too small in size for soup, and has not a long enough handle for toddy, so no doubt it was used for gravy, perhaps in one of those interesting "Old Blue" dishes made about 1800 and later, which had such deep wells in them. The deep dishes in this same figure were almost bowls, and took the place of vegetable-dishes.

In different places in this country I have found hot-water dishes made of pewter, for keeping food warm. They were almost like bowls, with a fixed dish in the top, and in this top or at one side was a little square bit of the pewter which could be withdrawn, so as to admit the water or pour it out. In Figure 23 is shown one of these, which belonged to William, the grandfather of Ralph Waldo Emerson. Mr. William Emerson built the "Old Manse" at Concord, Mass., which was celebrated through being the home of the Emerson family for so many years, and was further distinguished by sheltering Nathaniel Hawthorne, who, in an upper chamber, wrote some of those romances which have become a part of American classic literature. William Emerson, it is delightful to remember, was a patriot first and then a preacher, and no doubt was often late to his meals in those days when at every opportunity men met and talked about the imposition of England, and when every New England soul was awake and preparing to strike out for its own. How often did this dish repose on the hob while waiting for the goodman to come home! The coffee-urn was his too, but not the other cups, though in those days minister and ploughman alike took his N. E. rum more times a day than I like to set down, and never was seen the worse for it.

The tankard which stands modestly withdrawn into the background has quite a bit of romance connected with it, though its appearance is prosaic enough. It was owned originally by a retired sea-captain of Charlestown, Mass., who gave it, filled with gold coin, to his eldest daughter on her marriage. He also made the request that it should be handed down to her eldest daughter on her marriage, and so on, and that on

Fig. 22. CHARGERS, BOWLS, LADLE AND TASTER
Collection of Mr. William M. Hoyt

Fig. 23. COLLECTION OF PEWTER IN CONCORD, MASS.

every occasion it should be filled with gold coins. Unfortunately the family fortunes were on the top of the wave when the sea-captain's daughter was married, and though thrice or more times it has been handed down filled, it was with silver, not with gold, and the last time it passed it was quite empty, save with love and good wishes. This photograph and the history of the pieces shown in it were obtained for me by one who has now passed on. He was one of those kind souls who took an infinite deal of pains to help and be of service whenever it came in his power, and to his conscientious work I am indebted for many of the choice photographs which were taken for me of china, furniture, and pewter, in Concord and its neighbourhood.

One of the earliest and most important objects made in pewter was the candlestick. Torches made of pinewood or other inflammable material, stuck in a ring in the wall, was one means of lighting, the high-piled fire was another, and " early to bed " was put into practice oftener than it is now. In the Pewterers' Company's books the first mention of a " bell Candil-stikke " is in 1489. Several of these candlesticks are shown in Figure 24, each one of them having its grease-tray part way down its stem. The three to the left belong to one collection, and are much battered and marred, having been left as they were found many years ago in a moat, where they had been immersed in water for nobody knows how many years. They are extremely heavy, and designedly so, since it was necessary to make them firm enough to avoid the danger of having them tip over. The standard weights of candlesticks in 1612 were as follows:

Ordinarie highe candlesticks to weighe by peare,			03 lb,	00 qtr.	
Grete middle	"	"	"	02 "	" "
Smale	"	"	"	02 "	" "
Grete new fashion	"	"	"	03 "	" "
" bell	"	"	"	03 "	" "
Lowe bell	"	"	"	02 "	" "
Grete Wryteinge	"	"	"	01 "	" "
Smale Wryteinge	"	"	"	00 "	03 "
Grawnd with bawles	"	"	"	04 "	00 "
Ordinarie highe	"	"	"	03 "	00 "
Smale middle	"	"	"	02 "	" "

Throughout the sixteenth and seventeenth centuries the candlestick was of a somewhat dwarf pattern, consisting chiefly of a socket on a short neck, mounted on a heavy base. When, however, they began to be used on the table, they assumed greater height, and from about 1670 onward they grew rather taller and more ornate. The earliest of these tall candlesticks were copied from those used in the churches, which in turn took their shape from the cathedral pillar. The bases are heavy and generally dished, and somewhere on the stem is the grease-ledge. This lasted till 1708, when the ledge finally departed, leaving often an elementary ledge decorated with gadrooning in the higher-class candlestick, as seen in the second one from the left in Figure 25.

Domestic candlesticks were rarely more than nine inches in height, the tallest one in Figure 25 being but twelve inches. Of course those made for the guilds or city companies were very much taller, but these

Fig. 24. THREE CANDLESTICKS WITH BELL-SHAPED BASES
*From the Collection of S. Chisenhale Marsh. Esq.; the Fourth
from Messrs. Fenton & Sons*

hardly interest us, since they were commonly made of silver. The heavy candlestick fell more and more into disuse when something was required on the dining-table, and also on the still smaller tables which were used for cards in the reigns of William III and Anne. The columns became more slender, ornament was sparingly introduced, and the pewter sticks modestly followed the style set by those of finer metal.

There are items constantly occurring in the Pewterers' Books of sums paid to the "waxchaundeler" for torches and tapers supplied by him " at the buriing of Brethern and Sustren here bifore named and for the masse of our lady and for the makyng of the braunch at ii times wth iiij of newe wax," etc.

But such candles and candlesticks as these were for the prosperous middle classes, or even for those of higher rank. The poor people could not afford either candlesticks of such quality or the wax candles to burn in them. They had to be content with rushlights, and a special kind of holder came for these, specimens of which are very rarely found now, even in the remote cottage districts of England. I have never found one in America. Miss Jekyll, in her " Old West Surrey," says that we can hardly—

—"realise the troubles and difficulties in the way of procuring and maintaining artificial light for the long dark mornings and evenings of half the year, that prevailed among cottage folk not a hundred years ago. Till well into the third or fourth decade of the nineteenth century many labouring families could afford nothing better than the rushlights that they made at home, and these, excepting the firelight, had been their one means of lighting for all the preceding generations."

In the summer-time the children were sent into the marshy ground to gather the rushes, which were then at their full growth. The tough skin was peeled off, leaving the pith within, which was dried, the rushes being hung in bunches either out of doors or in the fireplace. Then all the fat that could possibly be spared was gathered, and melted down in grease-pans, which were pointed at each end and stood on three short feet among the ashes, which kept the grease melted. Eight or ten rushes at a time were drawn through this grease and then put aside to dry. The rushes were grasped in iron holders which held them upright between two jaws, and, when the light was new and long, a bit of paper was laid on the table to prevent the grease from spreading. Many were the devices practised by the cottagers to make the holders steady, the most common being to insert the holder, which was of the nature of a bit of iron bar with jaws at the top, into a heavy block of wood.

"Two pins crossed would put out a rushlight, and often cottagers going to bed—their undressing did not take long—would lay a lighted rushlight on the edge of an oak chest or chest of drawers, leaving an inch of light over the edge. It would burn up to the oak and then go out. The edges of old furniture are often found burnt into shallow grooves from this practice."

The candles which it was customary to use in the sticks shown in Figure 24 could not have been made of a very excellent quality of grease or wax, hence the necessity for a bracket to hold and catch it. More modern ones are shown in Figure 25, the fluted one coming under the head of "Queen Anne," and show-

Fig. 25. CANDLESTICKS OF VARIOUS TYPES

ing quite plainly that it has been cast in a silver mould. The oldest one of these is on the extreme left, and has a small grease-tray.

All these candlesticks are more ornate and delicate, if that word may be used in connection with pewter, than the ordinary run of such articles generally are. There is a certain solidity—I had almost said stolidity—in the alloy itself, which is not compatible with lightness, and the candlesticks of English make which were in use in that country and found their way over here were more like the examples given in Figure 26. These have no marks on them, and it is not known where they were made. They belonged to a collector in New Jersey, and are fine, well-preserved sticks. The photograph hardly does them justice, since it fails to show a fine engraving in four or five places on the stem, with milling on the three rings, and what looks like wriggled work around the bases. Such candlesticks as these held the choicest wax and dipped candles which the housewife could make. If possible she used bayberry-wax, which was highly esteemed from New Orleans to Canada. In 1705 Robert Beverley described it as follows:

"A pale brittle wax of a curious green colour, which by refining becomes almost transparent. Of this they make candles which are never greasy to the touch, never melt with lying in the hottest weather; neither does the snuff of these ever offend the smell like that of a tallow candle, but instead of being disagreeable if an accident puts a candle out, it yields a pleasant fragrancy to all that are in the room; insomuch that nice people often put them out on purpose to have the incense of the expiring snuff."

Long Island was one place where the bayberry-bushes grew in profusion, and they grow there still. There are one or two elderly people who make such candles as these yet, and some are for sale,—and they are fitting objects to burn in one of these old candlesticks of a summer evening.

By 1749 could be bought in Boston " Sperma Ceti candles," for they were advertised in the " Boston Independent Advertiser," and " Sweetness of Scent when extinguished, as well as Dimensions of Flame," were extolled as some of their merits.

One of the most important things in a household must have been its moulds for the making of candles. These moulds were often of pewter, and there were very definite rules as to their making, which shows that they were esteemed worthy of careful workmanship. We find this record :

" 1702. Thomas Greener appeared upon Sumons to this Court to give account of what Mettle he makes Candle Moulds And declared he made them of a mixture of Mettle something worse than pale and that they may be better of Fine But that he has experienced that they cannot be made of Lay. Thereupon this Court considering That the making of any new sort of Pewter vessel or Ware of any other sort of Mettle than perfectly fine or at the Assize of Lay may be of a very dangerous consequence And that there is great quantities of Candle Moulds now made of Mettle worse than Pale Though the same sorts of Moulds were first made of fine Pewter. That from henceforth it is ordered all Candle Moulds shall be made of Pewter perfectly fine And that the Maker thereof shall mark every such Mould tnat ne shall make with his own proper Mark or Touch."

Such moulds are to be met with from time to time in

Fig. 26. PEWTER CANDLESTICKS
Collection of Mr. A. Killgore

Fig. 27. CANDLE-MOULDS
Collection of the late Mrs. Merchant

America, and are for making two, four, six, or eight candles. Some that have seen long service are shown in Figure 27. The process of making such candles required skill on the part of the maker, but it was easier, and the product was better, than when they were dipped, which was truly back-breaking work. But the colonists had not been living long on American shores before they began to utilize the fish which swarmed in our waters, to produce oil. Francis Higginson, writing in 1630, says that though New England has "no tallow to make candles of, yet by abundance of fish thereof, it can afford oil for lamps."

In that most interesting record, Josselyn's "New England's Rarities," which was written between 1663 and 1671, I find this item with reference to oil:

"The Sperma Ceti whale differeth from the whales which yield us Whale-bones, for the first hath great and long teeth, the other nothing but Bones with tassels hanging from their Jaws, with which they suck in their prey."

While this account of the appearance of the whale is highly picturesque and is drawn largely from the writer's imagination, what follows seems to have been quite true.

"It is not long since a Sperma Ceti Whale or two were cast upon the shore not far from Boston in the Massachusetts Bay, which being cut up into small pieces and boyled in Cauldrons, yeilded plenty of Oyl; The Oyl put up in hogsheads, and stow'd into Cellars for some time, candies at the bottom, it may be one quarter; then the Oyl is drawn off, and the Candied stuff put into convenient vessels, is sold for Sperma Ceti, and is right Sperma Ceti."

This was no doubt used for candles, but that was not the only use to which it was applied, for he goes on to say that "the Oyl that was drawn off candies again and again if well ordered, and is admirable for Bruises and Aches."

In 1686 Governor Andros asked for a commission for a voyage for "Sperma Coeti Whales." In 1671 Nantucket, then known as Sherburne, began her whaling operations, and grew to be the greatest whaling town in the world, and oil for burning was soon in demand in all settled parts of this country. André Michaux, a Frenchman who came here in 1793 and went much about the country, wrote, on his return to France, a book which he called "Early Western Travels." It gives much information as to the struggles of the western pioneers. In 1802, F. A. Michaux, his son, continued the record, and I find that he has this to say with reference to petroleum:

"The Seneca Indian Oil in so much repute here is Petroleum; a liquid bitumen which oozes through fissures of the rocks and coal in the mountains, and is found floating on the surface of the water of several springs in this part of the country [near Pittsburg], whence it is skimmed off. It is very inflammable. In these parts it is used as a medicine, in external applications."

The most primitive form of lamp was the so-called Betty lamp, a specimen of which is shown in the chapter on brass. These lamps were never made of pewter. When the demand arose, it was not long before there were a number of styles to be had, which are shown in Figures 28 and 29. None of these lamps have any

Fig. 28. PEWTER LAMPS
Whipple House, Ipswich, Mass.

Fig. 29. OIL LAMP
National Museum, Washington

mark on them, and it is impossible to tell if they are of foreign or domestic make. The group of five are to be found at the Whipple House, Ipswich, Mass., and the single one is in Washington, D. C., and is among the articles which are said to have belonged at Mount Vernon in the days of George Washington. All of them are in excellent condition, and they are all less than eight inches high. The one at the extreme left has a thick glass magnifying arrangement, in the nature of a bull's-eye, which throws the light upon any object, much enlarged and brightened.

These lamps were not, however, the most primitive for burning oil, for in Figure 30 is shown an even more crude one. This seems but one remove from the rushlight or Betty lamp, and was probably used as a bedroom light. I have found them not only in pewter, but in Britannia ware as well, showing that their manufacture must have extended over a considerable length of time.

Much more uncommon were hanging lamps of pewter, yet such there were, and the one shown in Figure 31 could be utilised as a hand lamp as well, as it swung between two curved posts when not on duty on the wall. The more I see of pewter oil lamps, the more I am inclined to believe that many if not most of them were made in this country, since they are very rarely seen in either public or private collections abroad. Not one was shown at the exhibition of old pewter held in London about a year ago, and none of them are marked. I do not find any pewter lamps of any description mentioned in the lists of articles made by the Pewterers' Company at any time, and if they were in use they would surely be found there.

On the other hand it is not a difficult thing to find in England most interesting and sometimes handsome pewter saltcellars; and while we have some fine examples in silver in this country, notably the one at Harvard College, I have been obliged to go to London for illustrations of these useful articles. Three are given in Figure 32, all of them choice specimens, the one to the right having a peculiar interest for us, since it belongs to the fine collection of pewter gathered by Mr. De Navarro, who some years ago married Miss Mary Anderson, and whose house at Broadway, in England, has many rare and beautiful objects.

To-day, in our domestic economy, the saltcellar shares with the pepper-pot a position of importance on the table. Some hundreds of years ago it held undisputed sway, the pepper apparently being added in the kitchen, or very rarely, in the case of "standing salts," there was a top of pierced pewter where there was pepper. They were called "salers" before they were known as saltcellars, and in those delightfully picturesque but not wholly secure days, when poison was often used for the taking off of undesirables, the saltcellar was likely to be the receptacle for the fatal dose. Under these circumstances it is easy to see why they were often made with covers. In fact they were sometimes locked, or the cover could be chained down. Later they were furnished with one or two arms or brackets upon which were hung nap-

Fig. 30.   OIL LAMP
Collection of Mrs. David Hoyt

Fig. 31.   PEWTER GROUP
Collection of Mr. W. R. Lawshe

kins or cloths to protect the contents from meddlers and to keep it clean.

Standing salts are mentioned in wills by the beginning of the fourteenth century, but there are none of these very early ones to be found, even of silver. They were not of any particular design, but were fashioned to imitate lions, tigers, castles, dragons, elephants, or even human figures, and it was not till the middle of the fifteenth century that a definite shape was arrived at, which was something like an hour-glass or the letter X. By the sixteenth century the sides of the saltcellar became straight, and some of the finest of these standing salts had perforated covers for pepper. At the end of the sixteenth century the sides became concave, and ball feet were added, and they were known as " bell salts."

By the time of Charles the First and the Commonwealth, the standing salt, the position of which on the table indicated the relative social condition of the guests, since the nobles sat above it, and the retainers below it, ceased to have its former consequence. The lines of caste were less sharply drawn, sentiment was more republican, and symbols to define the differences between noble and commoner were no longer so rigorously demanded. For this reason the stately and elegant standing salt gave place to what was almost a reversion to the first type of the X-shape, and the cover was replaced by the napkin previously mentioned. By 1700 the form was very simple. For some time before this there had been a growing demand for " trencher salts," so called, quite small in size, which

were to be distributed among the guests. These plain
salt cellars remained in vogue during the whole eighteenth century, at least in pewter, though those of silver
took on varied fanciful forms which could not be
imitated in the baser metal.

The list of the possessions of the Pewterers' Company at their first Hall in 1489 is interesting, since
it was a prosperous guild and had many rooms com-
fortably furnished.

The members of the craft were called on for liberal
contributions, and the first gift was a table of " cipyrs "
(cypress) three yards long, and a " littl bord wth iiii
fete." One " pewtrer "—he must have been well to
do—gave " two sylur sponys iche of they hauing on
the endis a postell [apostle] wroght and ouergilt."
There were also brass pots, iron spits, and one " Bel
Candilstikke," a posnet of brass, four tables to play
upon, and a new ladder.

The next year one of the " bretheren " left to the
guild by will a stone mortar and pestie, a goblet,
basin, and three salts without covers. They had a
hard time getting their windows glazed in the great
hall, for glass was not a common commodity in 1490,
and they finally effected it by having each man do his
share, such an item being frequent as, " the midell
pane of the baye windowe glassid thurgh by Willm
Welby."

Forms, stools, and trestle-boards were the main
furniture, and there were many table-cloths and napkins including " A table cloth of diapre of ten yerde
long and two yerde brode of ye gifte of a peautrers

Fig. 32.   THREE SALTCELLARS

From the Collections of: 1. F. Inigo Thomas, Esq.   2. C. F. C.
Buckmaster, Esq.   3. A. F. DeNavarro, Esq.

wif nameles god reward hir." There were also specified, and particularly marked on the margin of the
book, a gift of eight " saltes of fyne metell wtout
coueryng weiyng six lbs., made of such metalle as ben
crossid vpon the heed bifore in this boke."

In 1612 the weights of saltcellars were set down in
this table:

	lb.	qtrs.
" Great duble bells wth pep. boxes and baules the half dozen to weighe	09.	00.
Greate duble Bells plaine, ha. doz.	06.	00.
Middle dubble wth bawles " "	06.	00.
Smale	03.	00.
Greate single	06.	00.
Smale single	02.	03.
The wrought Acorne salt	04.	00.
The greate Chapnut	01.	00.
Ye smale ye	01.	00.

Such salts as those shown in Figure 32 were made
in two or more pieces and then soldered together.
The bowl was one, and the foot the other piece. Round
ones are commoner than those with octagonal bases
and sides, since from the very nature of the alloy it
was easier to make them in this way. There is only
one set of octagonal plates and platters known, and
they are in England, and have been in the owner's
family for a hundred and fifty years, although not
in use for the last eighty.

I find by old letters and records that even by 1820
there were some old conservative families who still
used their pewter in those stately homes which even
yet line those long New England streets which we
know so well; and while the ladies saw to it that their

pewter was kept as bright as silver, the male members clung to their ruffled shirts and brass-buttoned coats.

Inkstands were another class of small objects which had a ready sale, and they were of different fashions,— one on a stand with a drawer beneath being shown on the left-hand side of the group which is shown in Figure 19. These did not wear very well, for they were easily bent. Another style consisted of a tray with an inkpot on it, as well as a box for sand. Far commoner were those small round pots without lids, of which an example is shown in Figure 31, standing next to the little whale-oil lamp. How often have the dried-up contents of such a pot been hastily inundated with water when Corydon or Phyllida took their infrequent pen in hand to answer or indite a *billet doux!*

Leather boxes for shaving-materials had pewter fittings and shaving-mug; I know of several of these, and of one in particular which was brought over by one of the French officers who accompanied La Fayette when he came to our assistance in 1776. In the soapbox is still a cake of soap, all dried up, but yet showing the mottoes with which it was decorated. It is needless to say that this red-leather box is treasured by its owner, who is one of the descendants of the officer who brought it to this country.

There are many references in the Pewterers' books to articles with " bawles," which were the round feet on which the object stood. In Figure 33 is a tray with such " bawles," a rare and quaint specimen. Just what its original use was is not evident, but it resembles

Fig. 33. PEWTER GROUP
Collection of Mrs. E. P. Smillie

Fig. 34. PEWTER AND BRITANNIA TEAPOTS
Collection of Mr. Dudley Hoyt

somewhat the *tazzi* which were so popular when the great Wedgwood potted, before 1795. The pottery *tazzi* had a single foot, but the dish part was shallow like this piece. It is in good condition, and an interesting piece. Next it is a lamp upheld by three hollow supports; this is also of good old pewter, but the three teapots and the pitcher come under the head of Britannia ware, though many collectors like to include such among their pewter articles. This group of pewter belongs to a collector who lives in Vermont, and who began to gather old and good things together long before the fancy had taken so many other people. She has a large house, and it is filled with fine old mahogany, old glass, brass, fine china, and all sorts of lovely things. In fact she is quite proud of the fact that there are only two new articles of furniture in the house, and she is careful never to reveal their identity.

While there were such things as pewter teapots, they were not very useful, for if they were stood among the hot ashes (or in later years upon the stove) they melted away. If they were even set upon the hob they were apt to be spoiled, and in the cold houses of a hundred or more years ago it was desirable to keep the victuals and drink as hot as possible.

In Figure 34 there is a group of five teapots, two of them of pewter (and these are easily to be distinguished by their plain outlines) and three of Britannia ware, the second from the left being a shape that was often used by Dixon & Sons for whole tea-sets. I myself have a sugar-bowl like it, marked 1825.

It grieves collectors very much to tell them that such pieces, particularly if marked with the names of either Dixon or Vickers, are not pewter. I had a letter not long since from a collector and dealer who said that he had handled thousands of pieces of pewter during the last few years, and that he owned a tea-set, marked Dixon, which was as good pewter as any pieces which he had ever seen. But neither Dixon nor Vickers ever made pewter; they were makers of " white metal " pure and simple, the credit of making pewter has been thrust upon them.

One of the commonest uses to which pewter was put was the fashioning of church vessels, and nearly all churches, if not richly or royally endowed, began with pewter communion-services, even if they did get rid of them as soon as they could or had them silver-plated. After the rude horns which had served for drinking-cups had been superseded by something better, the earthenware and glass which could be obtained was considered too perishable; wood had been forbidden; so gold, silver, and pewter remained. The cups, chalices, patens, and alms-plates of pewter were often enriched with engravings of Biblical scenes or mottoes. Sometimes even the font was made of this alloy, in which case it had to be of unusual thickness.

Perhaps it was fortunate that so many church vessels were made of pewter, for in this way they escaped confiscation at the dissolution of the monasteries in 1537; and after the Reformation, when communion was the rule, it was specified that " Wine we require to be brought to the Communion Table in a clean and

Fig. 35.   CHURCH FLAGON, DATED 1753
Collection of Dr. H. Tait

sweet standing pot or stoup of pewter." This was in 1603. The subject of "Church Plate" has interested antiquarians in England during the last few years, and in Nightengale's "Church Plate of Dorset" the earliest flagons described are dated 1641, while in Andrew Trollope's "Church Plate of Leicestershire" are mentioned flagons dated from the year 1635. The last pieces purchased which are mentioned in this latter inventory were dated 1800.

The shapes of the flagons varied somewhat, and they were to be found with a spout or not, more frequently without, and in Figure 35 is shown a handsome example dated 1735 and in excellent preservation. It is sixteen inches high, though many of them were only eleven to fourteen, and I have seen a flagon designated as "great" which was but thirteen inches tall. The types of cups were like the one in Figure 36, which is of the shape known as "Presbyterian," and which is still in use in Scotland, where pewter for church use has survived longer than anywhere else.

The Scotch guild of Pewterers was a very important body, and, like those of England, had very rigid rules by which they were governed. They were not organised as early as were their English brethren, since it was 1496 before the hammermen became of sufficient importance to have a "seal of cause," or charter, granted to them in Edinburgh, which was the most important town in Scotland at that time. But for a century, or a little less, little pewter was made, for its price was so great that only the wealthy could afford it, and they obtained what they needed from France and England..

The rules and regulations of the Scotch guild are much like the English ones.

"1. That no hammerman or servant presume to practise more arts than one, to prevent damage or hurt to other trades.

"2. That no person presume to expose for sale any sort of goods in the street at any other time than the market day.

"3. That persons best qualified of each of the crafts be empowered to search for and inspect the goods made, and if found insufficient in material and workmanship, a fine to be imposed.

"4. That all hammermen be examined by the masters and deacons of their several crafts, and if their essays be found good they were to be admitted freemen of the Incorporation.

"5. That no person harbour or employ the servant or apprentice of another without the master's consent.

"6. That no one not of the aforesaid craft sell or vend any sort of work made by any other craft.

"7. That any persons guilty of breaking any of these above articles pay eight shillings Scots."

The Scotch pewterers' craft, in common with all others, had two masters, who looked after the interests of their guild, saw to the admission of apprentices, who became freemen after serving an apprenticeship of seven years, and examined the admission-pieces made by applicants, such as lavers, basins, and flagons, the article changing from year to year till in 1794 a three-pound dish and a pint flagon were all that were required, since the palmy days of pewter had passed, and it was being crowded out by both pottery and tinware, either of them cheaper substitutes.

The "Whiteironsmiths," as the tin-workers were called, were at odds with the pewterers almost from

Fig. 36.   COMMUNION CUP, "PRESBYTERIAN"

the beginning, and though at first they worked under the jurisdiction of the guild of Hammermen, by 1739 they were anxious to form a guild by themselves. This was promptly denied them by the pewterers, and the two sets of workers hung together, always jealous of each other, and ready to report any infringements of each others' rights.

The matter of stamping was under the same regulations as in England, and each piece was to be marked with the maker's private mark as well as with the quality mark and the small imitation hall marks. The maker's mark often included his name, and one of the hall marks was generally the thistle, which has now come to be one of the chief distinguishing marks of Scotch pewter. Unfortunately their "touch-plates" have entirely disappeared, if ever there were any, and it is often difficult to tell the difference between pieces of English and Scotch make. There are marks of the different cities, however, but they are seldom present except on flagons. They are such marks as the one of Edinburgh (which shows a triple-towered castle standing on a rock, a tree, fish, and bird on tree) and the bell of Glasgow.

There was a certain "Johnny Faa," a gypsy king who was granted the title of "Lord and Count of Little Egypt," and his dependents or followers seem to have been travelling pewterers or tinkers, who went about the country recasting old and broken pewter. These men were required to have a license, and a set of these licenses dating from 1600 to 1764, bearing initials and dates, are now preserved in the Antiquarian Museum of Scotland. There is also a list of the Freemen belonging to the Incorporation of Hammermen from 1600 to 1800, recording the dates of their admission to the guild, the recurrence of certain names showing how the trade descended from father to son, and even to grandson.

The Scottish pewter, like the English, never revelled in that wealth of ornament which was bestowed on it by the Continental pewterers. It was simple and dignified in outline, and susceptible of use for domestic purposes, what decoration it had being confined to mouldings and some slight engraving.

Perhaps the favourite of all the Scotch utensils was the drinking-vessel which went by the curious name of "tappit-hen" (see Figure 37), and which could be so small that it would hold but a pint, or large enough to hold three quarts. The larger sizes were really confined to tavern use, and they commonly had a small cup fastened just within the lid. These great vessels were brought to the doors of travelling-coaches, which were the only means of locomotion on land in those days, and the weary and exhausted travellers, each in his turn, might refresh and warm themselves with the strong drink, which was piping hot when it came from the tap-room of the inn. Sir Walter Scott refers to these drinking-vessels in " Waverley," when he says:

"The hostess appeared with a large pewter measure containing at least three English quarts, familiarly denominated a 'tappit-hen.'"

There was another style of drinking-vessel that was

Fig. 37. "TAPPIT-HENS"

called a " quaich," and which was nearly identical with the two-eared bowls which were so common in England and Holland, and which have already been shown (Figure 21). The chief difference lay in the handles, the Scotch ones being solid, while those of English or Continental make had the handles pierced in different patterns. The size of these quaiches ran from three to nine inches across, the former being used as a drinking-cup, many of them being in use in remote parishes till within recent years. The larger-sized ones were porridge-bowls, and in them was served the " parritch," the favourite dainty of every true Scotsman.

The thrifty Scot was in the habit of saving his pennies when he could, and for this purpose a little money-box of earthenware was made, which was known by the quaint name of " the Pirley Pig." One of these boxes made of pewter (Figure 38) is called the " most curious piece of pewter in Scotland." It belongs to the Town Council of Dundee, and is in shape like an orange a little flattened. It is but three inches high and six in diameter, and on one side is an opening through which an iron rod passes, to fasten it in its place, so that it could not be stolen. On the opposite side is a slit through which the money was dropped, and this box was used to receive the fines of those members of the Council who failed to attend the meetings. As may be seen, it was finely decorated, and has on it the royal arms as well as those of " Sir James Skrimzeour, Prowest, Anno 1602, 14 May." The history of this fine little piece of work was like that of so many other relics,—it was rescued from a heap of waste as lately as 1839, after being lost for many years and having escaped the melting-pot, that awful pit which swallowed up so much pewter.

The pewter beggars' badges were in use in Scotland longer than in any other country, for they were issued as lately as the middle of the last century. Sometimes the name of the beggar was inscribed on the badge, sometimes the arms of the town, while in other instances there was only a number, with the name of the town and parish.

In the Museum of Antiquities at Edinburgh there is a circular badge of pewter, about the size of a half-dollar, which has on it a crowned thistle and the initials V.R., with the date 1847, the number 28, and the name "William Bain," following which are the words "Pass and Repass." This was probably one of the last of these badges which was issued.

Communion-tokens were a feature of the Scottish Churches, both Episcopalian and Presbyterian. While they were made of pewter they were quaint in design and of various shapes. The first one that is on record is spoken of in a Glasgow Sessions Record for 1593. This one was, no doubt, lead, for pewter was by no means common in Scotland at that date. Later, however, they were made of pewter, and by the churches that issued them, so that no maker's mark ever appeared on them.

The shapes were very various, I have seen them of heart design as well as square, octagonal, and round. First they bore only the initial letter of the parish to which the holder belonged; then some small ornament was added, like a star, or a tree; and then came a date. The use of them continued till the middle of the nineteenth century, when the pewter tokens were replaced by cardboard tickets.

The way in which these tokens were used seems strange enough to us now, and was confined to Scotland. On a week-day, those who wished to partake of communion presented themselves before the minister and elders and received one of these tokens, which had to be given up on Sunday before the possessor could obtain communion. They were given out in no indiscriminate manner, for if sought by a person who was known to be evil in ways of living it was denied. This, as may be imagined, led to many hot scenes at the distribution, so that it became general for the minister to examine each applicant first, lest refusal might prove necessary. These communion-tokens are smaller than the beggars' badges, probably for convenience in carrying in the hand, while the badges were worn on the outside of the coat so that they could be easily seen.

In America the most common pieces of pewter to be found are those for domestic use, although I know of portions, at least, of communion-services which have been rescued from ignominy by collectors. There are also some sets which are retained by the parishes which originally owned them, and which, though no longer in use, are respectfully treated in consideration of their one-time service. In 1729 the First Church at Hanover, Mass., bought a set of communion-vessels and a christening-basin, all of pewter. It still preserves them as relics. Grafton, Mass., has another set, five pieces in all,—two flagons, two patens, and a tankard,—inscribed as the gift of one of the deacons of the church in 1742. These are also carefully preserved, but I know of another set, also inscribed, which was rescued from a peddler's wagon, where it had been thrown as " junk " in exchange for new tinware.

How late these communion-services continued to be used among our country churches it would be hard to say, yet in the records of the First Church of Rockingham, Vt., for March 22, 1819, I find this entry with regard to the purchase of a pewter communion-service:

" Whereas it is very desirable, by every well-wisher to every religious institution, that every necessary and decent provision for the accommodation and utility of its members should be made; and whereas we, the subscribers, understand that the Sacramental Table, in the Congregational Meeting-house in this town, is now and ever has been wholly unfurnished with suitable vessels for the decently and conveniently celebrating the Gospel Institution of The Lord's Supper; Therefore, we, the undersigned, severally engage to pay to Mr. Royal Earl the sum annexed to our respective names for the sole purpose of purchasing all necessary furniture for said Table. The said furniture, purchased as aforesaid, shall be the sole property of the Congregational Church, for their public use and benefit for ever."

Then follow the names of 44 subscribers, the largest amount given being $2.50 and the smallest 20 cents. The total amount subscribed was $28.74, and then comes this additional note, which reflects that credit on the Female Society that one ever looks for in those circumstances where something is needed to fill a gap in the church or parish, and which has been overlooked by the masculine minds which have first say, but do not always speak to the point, though I know it is heresy to say so!

"In addition to the foregoing, the Female Society advanced three dollars and purchased the Baptismal Bason. Mrs. Eunice Richards gave the Table cloth and Two Small napkins or Towels. The whole furniture, in addition to the foregoing, consists of two large Tankard Pots, four cups, two with handles, and two small Platters."

Then, in a different hand, follow—

"*Directions for cleansing the foregoing vessels.* Take a piece of fine woollen cloth, upon this put as much sweet oil as will prevent its rubbing dry; with these rub them well in every part; then wipe them smartly with a soft dry linen rag, and then rub them off with soft wash leather and whiting. N. B. If convenient, wash them in boiling water and soap, just before they are rubbed with wash-leather and whiting. This would take off the oil more effectually, and make the engraving look brighter."

Can you not see the Female Society planning to spend that three dollars out of their small treasury, and then considering all the ways of cleaning pewter, the majority settling on the rules set down above? I have tried to find out if this set is still in existence, but no replies have been received to my letters, though they were never returned.

While the use of pewter lasted long in the churches whose members were not burdened by world's gear, in the large cities, at least, where other wares could be obtained, its use for domestic purposes was being superseded. It had held its own in America for two hundred years and over; for, from the very nature of the material, it was good to carry in the scant baggage brought over by the pioneers, since about the worst that could happen to it was a few dents, which could be hammered out if they were too deep or if they threatened to injure the usefulness of the vessel.

From almost the very first there are plenty of records of pewter. In 1647, when the widow Coytemore married John Winthrop, she brought to him, from the estate of her late husband, pewter valued at £135.

In 1657 Governor William Bradford died. He left an inventory of so much and such valuable property that I am going to give it all, since it is often misquoted and is never given entire. The family of Governor Bradford included himself and wife and two children. Then there were the Rogers, Latham, and Cushman boys, who fell to the charge of Governor Bradford on the deaths of their parents. A little later, Mrs. Kempton, who was related to the governor, came into the family, and she brought her four children with her, and her husband as well, so that there were thirteen in the family to be provided for. This inventory is transcribed from the Plymouth Records, and it is unfortunate that so many of the articles have disappeared.

" Bedding and other things in ye old parlor.

Impr. One feather bed and bolster; a feather bed a feather bolster a feather pillow; a canvas bed with feathers and a bolster and 2 pillows; one green rug; a paire of whit blanketts; 1 whit blankett; 2 pairs of old blanketts; 2 old coverlids; 1 old whit rugg and an old kid coverlid; 1 paire of old curtaines darnicks and an old paire of sach curtaines; a court cubbard; a winescot bedsteed and a settle; 4 lether chaires; 1 great lether chaire; 2 great wooden chaires; a table and a forme and 2 stooles; a winscott chist and cubbard; a case with six knives; 3 matchlock musketts; a snapchance muskett; a birding piece and a small piece; a pistoll and cutlas; a card and a plat.

In the great Rome.

2 great carved chaires; a smale carved chaire; a table and a forme; 3 striped carpetts; 10 cushions; 3 old cushens; a causlett and one head peece; 1 fouling peece without a locke; 3 old barrels of guns one paire of old bandeleers and a crest.

Linnin.

2 paire of holland sheets; 1 dowlis sheet; 2 paire of cotton and linnen sheets; 2 paire of hemp and cotten sheets; 2 paire of canvas sheets; 2 paire of old sheets; 4 fine shirts; 4 other shirts; a dozen of cotten and linnin napkins; a dozen of canvas napkins; a diaper tablecloth and a dozen of diaper napkins; 10 diaper napkins of another sort a diaper tablecloth; 2 holland tablecloths; 2 short tablecloths; 2 old tablecloths; a dozen of old napkins; halfe a dozen of napkins; 3 old napkins; a dozen of course napkins and a course tablecloth; 2 fine holland cubburd clothes; 3 paire of holland pillow beers; 3 paire of dowlis pillow beers and an old one; 4 holland towells and a lockorumone.

Pewter.

14 pewter dishes weying 47 pound att 15 d. a pound; 6 pewter plates and 13 pewter platters weying thirty pounds att 15 d. a pound; 2 pewter plates 5 sawsers 4 basons and 5 dishes weying eighteen pounds att 15 d. a pound; 2 py plates of pewter; 3 chamber potts; 7 porrengers; 2 quart potts and a pint pott; 2 old flagons an a yore; a pewter candlesticke a salt and a little pewter bottle; 4 venice glasses and seaven earthen dishes; 2 ffrench kittles.

In kitchen brasse.

1 brasse kittle; 2 little ffrench kittles; an old warming pan; 2 old brasse kittles; a dash pan; 3 brasse skillets; 3 brasse candle stickes and a brassemorter and pestle; an old brasse skimmer and a ladle; a paire of andirons an old brasse stewpan; 2 old brasse kittles; 2 iron skillets and an iron kittle; 2 old iron potts; 2 iron potts lesser; 2 paire of pot hangers and 2 paire of pott hookes; 2 paire of tongges and an old fier shouel; one paire of andirons

and a gridiron; a spitt and an old iron driping pan; a paire of iron racks and an iron peele and another peec of old iron to lay before a driping pan; 4 dozen of old trenchers; 2 juggs and 3 smale bottles.

In the new chamber his clothes.

A stuffe suite with silver buttons and a coate; a cloth cloake faced with taffety lineed threw with baies; a sod coullered cloth suite; a turkey Grogorum suite and a cloake; a paire of black britches and a kid wastcoat; a lead coullered cloth suit with silver buttons; a sod coullered short coate and an old serge suite; a blacke cloth coate; a broad cloth coate; a light coullered stuffe coate; an old green goune; a light collered cloth cloake; an old violett coullered cloake; a short coate of cloth; 2 old dublett and a paire of briches a short coate and an old stuffe dublit and a wast-coate; 2 paire of stockens; 2 hates a black one and a coullered one; 1 great chaire and 2 wrought stooles; a carved chist; a table;

The Plate.

One great beer bowle; another great beer bowle; 2 wine cups; a salt; the trencher salt; and a drame cup; 4 silver spoones; 9 silver spoones.

In the Studdie.

8 paire of shoes of the 12 s.; 6 paire of shoes of the 10 s.; one paire of the eights; 3 paire of the sixes; 1 paire of the fives 1 paire of the 4s. 1 paire of the 3s.; 4 yards and a half of linnen woolcye; 3 remnants of English cotten; 3 yards and a halfe of bayes; 17 yards of course English moheer; 4 yards and 3 quar-ters of purpetuanna; 18 yards of kid penistone; 5 yards of broad-cloth; 2 yards of broadcloth; 2 and one half yards of olive cul-lered carsye; a yard and a halfe of whitish carsye; 4 yards of Gray carsye; 5 yards and a halfe of kid carsye; 4 yards and a quarter of carsey ollive coullered; 7 yards of carsay sod coul-iered; 6 yards of kid plaine; 9 yards and a halfe of kid plaine; 6 yards of holland; a remnant of cushening; 7 smale moose skins; in cash £151 9s. 6d.; his deske; 2 casks with some empty bottles; 3 or 4 old cases."

Then comes the list of his books, largely religious, and of the live stock, and items of what was owing the estate, over three hundred pounds, and the list of the " parcells " of land.

Even at this date the estate seems a worthy one, as indeed it had need to be to care for so many people.

Long Island had some settlers of means, and when Thomas Sayre died in 1669 at Southampton, he left his son Francis real estate and " a Pewter Flagon, a Pewter Bowl, and a great Pewter Platter." The house of this same Thomas Sayre is still standing, and is now the oldest house in the State.

In 1681 the inventory of Nathaniel Sylvester, of Shelter Island, was filed; among other things he leaves two hundred and eighty pounds of pewter valued at £14, one Turkey-wrought carpet £1. 10s., and one-half Shelter Island, valued at £700.

In 1676 James Briggs, of Scituate, complained that Constable Jenkins had taken from his house a pewter basin without first making a legal demand for his claim. The court ordered Jenkins to pay sixpence damages, and costs, and to restore the basin, or to pay seven shillings in silver as an equivalent. The basin must have been a fine one, as at that time money had four times its present value.

There was filed in Boston an inventory of a pew-terer who had in his shop 2,782 pounds of pewter, which, with the dishes and basins in stock, was valued at £235 11s. 4d. He had in addition alchemy spoons, spooning pewter, tankards, milk-cans, warming-pans, kettles, skillets, frying-pans, cow-bells, and bellows,—these latter of copper and brass.

One of the most frequently made, and yet one of the least common objects to find now, is a pewter spoon. The reason is not far to seek, since, besides the visiting tinker who melted down all broken pewter and then recast it, there was hardly a village where some family did not own a mould for re-running their spoons. Of course they were willing to lend it to their neighbours, and there is one town on record where all the spoons in it were marked with the same letter, since the family who owned the mould had on the handle the letter " L," the initial of their last name.

The spoon is an article so venerable that for its first mention one has to seek out Egyptian records. A shell is supposed to have suggested its first shape. The earliest step in its development was to mount this shell on a handle, and it is interesting to observe that in the Connecticut valley the early settlers inserted a clam-shell into a cleft stick, and found that this answered all the purposes for which spoons were made. The second step in the history of the spoon's growth was to fashion the whole object in one piece,—it mattered not whether it was made out of bone, wood, or metal; while during the fanciful and elegant Renaissance, rare shells, glass, ivory, and agate bowls were attached to handles of metal set with jewels or delicately wrought of silver or gold.

The earlier the spoon, the more nearly the bowl approaches the shape of the plover's egg, the pointed end being toward the handle. In the very early spoons the bowl was below the level of the handle, but by the fifteenth century this difference of levels had disappeared. The handles in Gothic times were square-sided, the tops terminating in an ornament like an acorn, or a diamond knob, a lion's or a human head, and even such whole figures as those of the Apostles, and finally what was known as the " seal-top," on which the initials of the owner could easily be cut. From 1550 to 1680 the seal-top spoon was the most common pattern, although the Apostle spoon also held its own. A complete set of these consisted of thirteen spoons, with the Master spoon in addition to the twelve Apostles. On many of the spoons in the last half of the sixteenth century the figures were removed to meet the rigid ideas of the new Protestant religion, and later this fashion was revived by the Puritans.

Within the last few months one of these spoons in pewter has been recovered from the bottom of the Thames, at London. The bowl is of the plover's-egg shape, but instead of having on the top an Apostle's figure it is ornamented with a woman's head dressed in the fashion of the early part of the fifteenth century, when the hair was arranged in two horns, over which was a head-dress of gold thread and jewels. The head of the spoon is still in good condition, and the spoon dates to the time of Henry V (1413-1422). Three more examples of this kind of spoon are known, one of which is in the British Museum.

The form of the spoon does not lend itself much to decoration, and when all known devices for ornamenting the handle had been exhausted, a novelty from

France was introduced by Charles II about 1665, and was eagerly welcomed. This necessitated an entire change in the whole form of the spoon: the bowl became an oval; the handle was made quite flat, and the top of it was broadened out and cleft into a rude resemblance to a hind's foot. The shape was called in France, "pied de biche," while, for no apparent reason, it was known in England as the "fish-tail." The bowls of these spoons are level with the handle, and are made strong where the handle joins the bowl, by a continuation of the handle, which is known as a "rat-tail."

In the beginning this rat-tail was contrived for strength only, and was perhaps suggested by the combined fork and spoon. This object had a movable spoon-bowl which fitted into the handle of the fork, the prongs of which folded back out of the way. The tail was a very ornamental feature in the early spoons, being beaded and decorated in various ways, and such spoons continued to be made down to Queen Anne's reign, when little by little the fish-tail on the handle was omitted, the bowl became deeper, and the handle was rounded forward and took the shape to which we are accustomed. The rat-tail was first seen about 1660 and lasted seventy or eighty years, when at length its place was taken by a simple scroll, and the bowl became pointed as in the modern spoon.

Two spoons are shown in Figure 39. The one with the round bowl came from Ghent and is marked H.K. in the crown, which is above a rose. It is the finest piece of pewter I have ever seen. It has a smoothness

Fig. 38. THE PIRLEY PIG

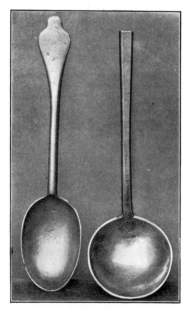

Fig. 39. PEWTER SPOONS
Belonging to the writer

to the touch, and takes a brilliancy of polish, which are not often found. Its bowl is hammered, the handle squared, and running down over the bowl is a heavy rat-tail. Its period is about 1700, and it was not of the small size which we use now, for its bowl measures two and a half inches across, and the handle is six inches long.

The other spoon has the exact shape as to handle and bowl which was in use in silver about 1710, but is of a later period than this. It has no mark except a blurred star in the bowl, there is a large preponderance of lead in its composition, and it is rough in every way. It came from Kennebunkport, Me., and is possibly eighty or one hundred years old and of domestic make. It was probably run in a mould taken from a silver spoon, these articles being somewhat rare in the equipment of the colonists. Anyone who had a silver spoon was no doubt willing to lend it for the purpose of making a plaster mould from which an iron or brass mould could be made, the former metal being generally used, though there were some of brass. I have seen both.

There were no pewter forks, for the alloy was not stiff enough to make it available. But their lack troubled our ancestors little; fingers and the blade of the knife were enough for them, and the first dated set of English silver forks were of the year 1667, though there were single forks before this. The lack of these utensils explains the abundance of napery which we find in all old inventories. Observe how much Governor Bradford had. It also explains the presence of that bowl known as the " rose-water dish," which in silver was choicely engraved and decorated, while in pewter it was most often but a simple bowl, either with or without some wriggled work or·engraving on it.

One of the great uses to which pewter was put in America as well as England was for vessels for tavern use. Sleeping-accommodations might be scant enough, but there were drinking-vessels enough for the men of the neighbourhood who gathered there, and for the occasional traveller, and tankards, mugs, beakers, and hot-water cans are frequently mentioned.

The " Black Horse Tavern," of Salem, Mass., was a famous one in its day, and when William Trask, its owner, died in 1691, he left the following property:

	£	s.	d.
Impr. A dwelling house, 1 barn, one orchyard and marsh adjoyning	110	00	00
Parlour. 1 standing bedsted & fether bed & beding	6	00	00
1 trundle bedsted, fether bed & beding	4	00	00
1 long table & forme		12	00
1 Cupbord in the Parlor, 8 chairs, 1 wainscot chist, and box, warming pan........................	1	10	00
Weareing apparel, 1 pr Irons & tongs, 12 glass bottles, 1 psle flax & yarn	8	05	00

Goods in Kitchen.

Brass & Pewter. 2 Iron potts, Prp. Iron doggs, 2 hakes pr tongs, grid iron fryeing pan & spitt.

In the Chambers.

1 old fether bed & beding, 12 yds new homemade cloth bcoks.

To his share in Mill.

5 acres of upland in ye north field, etc.

It may be seen from this how few travellers it was expected that the innkeeper should entertain over night, and indeed there was small profit in such business at first, since the landlord had to give to the selectmen the names of all such strangers as wished for " vitals, beare and lodgen," and if their credentials were not satisfactory they were warned from the town. The records of the old towns, particularly of those in New England, are bristling with rules and regulations as to the privileges of the landlord, the prices he could ask for his goods, and the guests he could entertain. For he could not " knowingly harbour in house, barn, or stable, any rogues, vagabonds, thieves, sturdy beggars, masterless men or women," and those delightful busybodies, the selectmen, decreed how much he should charge for every meal, as well as for each cup of sack or strong waters.

Two wills which are of peculiar interest to all Americans are given in the following pages, as they are valuable records of what composed the property of the well-to-do Virginia family in the first and last quarters of the eighteenth century. The first is that of Mrs. Mary Hewes, the grandmother of General George Washington, and it is dated 1721. The second comes nearer to our greatest hero, and is the will of his mother, an elegant old lady about whom Sparks started many stories which have no more truth in them than the famous " cherry-tree tale." The will of Mrs. Washington was dated 1788, and shows what an advance had been made in sixty-seven years in the comfort and convenience of our dwellings and their equipment. Pewter holds its own in both wills, as may be seen, and it was still accounted a valuable asset, since Mrs. Washington mentions it specifically and considers half of what she had enough for one bequest. The will of Mrs. Hewes leaves to her daughter, Mary Ball, the best part of her estate, although there were other children by another husband. There were elegances provided for the young girl, and her education was to be looked after, as befitted one of gentle birth. The will can speak for itself.

"First, I give and bequeath my soul to God that gave it me, and my body to the Earth to be buried in Decent Christian burial at the discretion of my executors in these presents nominated. And as touching such Worldly estate which it hath pleased God to bestow upon me, I give, devise and dispose of in the following manner and form.

Imprimis, I give and devise unto my Daughter Mary Ball one young likely negro woman to be purchased for her out of my Estate by my Executors, and to be delivered unto her the said Mary Ball at the age of eighteen years, but, my will is that if the said Mary Ball should dye without Issue lawfully begotten of her body, that the same negro woman and her increase shall return to my loving son John Johnson, to him, his heirs and assigns for ever.

"*Item.* I give and bequeath unto my said Daughter Mary Ball one young mare and her increase which said mare I formerly gave her by word of mouth.

"*Item.* I give and bequeath unto my said daughter Mary Ball two gold rings, the one being a large hoop and the other a stoned ring.

"*Item.* I give and bequeath unto my said daughter Mary Ball sufficient furniture for the bed her father Joseph Ball left her, vizt; One suit of good curtains and fallens, one Rugg, one Quilt, one pair Blanketts.

"*Item.* I give and bequeath unto my said daughter Mary Ball two diaper table cloths marked M. B. with inck, and one

Fig. 40. EWER AND BASIN
Collection of the late Mrs. Merchant

dozen of Diaper napkins, two towels, six plates, two pewter dishes, two basins, one large iron pott, one Frying pan, one old trunk.

"*Item.* I give and bequeath unto my said daughter Mary Ball, one young Paceing horse together with a good silk plush side saddle to be purchased by my Executors out of my estate.

"*Item.* I give and bequeath to my daughter Elizabeth Bonum one suit of white and black callico, being part of my own wearing apparel.

"*Item.* All the rest of my wearing apparel I give and bequeath unto my said Daughter Mary Ball, and I do hereby appoint her to be under Tutilage and Government of Captain George Eskridge, during her minority.

"*Item.* My will is I do hereby oblige my Executors to pay to the proprietor or his agent for the securing of my said Daughter Mary Ball her land Twelve pounds if so much be due.

"*Item.* All the rest of my Estate real and personal whatsoever and wheresoever, I give and devise unto my son John Johnson, and to his heirs lawfully begotten of his body, and for default of said Issue, I give and bequeath the said Estate unto my Daughter Elizabeth Bonum, her heirs and assigns forever.

"*Item.* I do hereby appoint my son John Johnson and my trusty and well beloved friend George Eskridge, Executors of this my last will and Testament and also revoke and Disannul all other former wills or Testaments by me heretofore made or caused to be made either by word or writing, ratifying and confirming this to be my last Will and Testament and no other.

In witness whereof I have hereunto sett my hand and seal the Day and Date at first above written.

"The mark and seal of Mary III Hewes. Sig. [Seal.]

"Signed, Sealed and Published and Declared by Mary Hewes to be her last Will and Testament in presence of us.

               "The mark of Robert X Bradley.

               "The mark of Ralph X Smithhurst.

                   "David Straughan."

Mrs. Mary Washington [the Mary Ball mentioned above] was a notable housekeeper and looked well after the ways of her household. She had some handsome furniture, more silver than was usual in even Virginia homes of that date, and when she died in 1788 her will, which was registered in the Clerk's Office at Fredericksburg, Va., shows how much she had to bequeath.

"In the name of God! Amen! I, Mary Washington of Fredericksburg, in the County of Spotssylvania, being in good health, but calling to mind the uncertainty of this life, and willing to dispose of what remains of my Worldly Estate, do make and publish this, my last will, recommending my soul into the hands of my Creator, hoping for a remission of all my sins through the merits and mediation of Jesus Christ, the Saviour of mankind; I dispose of my worldly estate as follows:

"Imprimis. I give to my son General George Washington, all my land in Accokeek Run, in the County of Stafford, and also my negro boy George, to him and his heirs for ever. Also my best bed, bedstead and Virginia cloth curtains (the same that stands in my best bedroom), my quilted blue and white quilt and my best dressing glass.

"Item. I give and devise to my son Charles Washington, my negro man Tom, to him and his assigns forever.

"Item. I give and devise to my daughter Betty Lewis, my phaeton and my bay horse.

"Item. I give and devise to my daughter-in-law Hannah Washington, my purple cloth cloak lined with shag.

"Item. I give and devise to my grandson, Corbin Washington, my negro wench old Bett, my riding chair, and two black horses, to him and his assigns for ever.

"Item. I give and devise to my grandson Fielding Lewis, my negro man Frederick, to him and his assigns for ever, also eight silver table spoons, half of my crockery-ware, and the blue and white tea china, with bookcase, oval table, one bedstead, one pair sheets, one pair blankets and white cotton counterpaine, two table cloths, six red leather chairs, half of my peuter, and one half of my kitchen furniture.

"Item. I give and devise to my grandson Lawrence Lewis, my negro wench Lydia, to him and his assigns forever.

"Item. I give and devise to my granddaughter Bettie Curtis,

Fig. 41.   AMERICAN PEWTER PITCHER
Collection of Mr. Baldwin Coolidge

my negro woman little Bett, and her further increase, to her and her assigns forever. Also my largest looking-glass, my walnut writing-desk and drawers, a square dining-table, one bed, bedstead, bolster, one pillow, one pair sheets one blanket and counterpain.

"Item. I devise all my wearing apparel to be equally divided between my granddaughters Bettie Curtis and Fannie Ball, and Milly Washington, but should my daughter Bettie Lewis fancy any one or two or three articles, she is to have them before division thereof.

Lastly I nominate and appoint my said son General George Washington, executor of this my will, and as I owe few or no debts, I direct my executor to give no security or appraise my estate, but desire that the same may be allotted to my devises, with as little trouble and delay as may be desiring their acceptance there of, as all the token I now have to give them of my love for them.

"In witness thereof I have hereunto set my hand and seal, the 20th. day of May, 1788.

Mary Washington."

In some of the inventories and records which I have quoted, mention is made of ewers and basins, but they do not always seem to be part of the same set. There were such sets, however, sometimes consisting of other objects besides the ewers and basins, and I find that many of these sets were made in America. It is most difficult to tell how much and what forms of pewter were made here, since there were no regulations regarding the making of it; no standard of fineness to be kept up, as there was abroad; and any journeyman tinker who had the tools and the moulds could re-run it. Of course on such pieces there would be no mark. Then the Revolution came along, and what pewter was not absolutely demanded for daily use was cheerfully given up and cast into the melting-pot, to be run into bullets. The ardent patriot who rocked the cradle went to the limit of her power to give, and even at a pinch gave up those articles which she had deemed indispensable, and their places were filled by bowls and trenchers of wood, which were whittled out by the boys and young men, and smoothed down by the active hands of the women, and polished by being rubbed with broken glass and sand. " Knot bowls " were held in much esteem in Revolutionary times, and there were men who made a business of making them, the persons who wished the articles generally furnishing the knots, which were preferably from apple-wood.

In " The Collector's Manual " I have spoken of the use to which the lead statue of George III, which stood on Bowling Green, New York city, was put, and lead roofs went the same way, the call for bullets always being cheerfully responded to,—even the lead plates on tombstones being pried out and melted up. Ewers and basins were perhaps considered among the frills which could be easily dispensed with, since the well always remained at hand, and there was too much good pewter in these articles to escape. Only a few have come down, and an ewer and basin in good order are shown in Figure 40. The ewer held about a gallon, and the basin was of that tiny pattern which was so closely followed by the makers of Old Blue china. It looks absolutely infantile in these days of generous toilet sets. The basin in this set is a fine piece, made according to the English rule, and well hammered, the marks of the mallet showing plainly in the photo-

Fig. 42. AMERICAN PEWTER. REED AND BARTON. EARLY NINETEENTH CENTURY

graph. These pieces are unmarked, but there are others scattered about the country, and generally the ewer and basin have become separated. I find more ewers than basins.

Many of these pieces are marked " Boardman," some of them " Thomas Boardman," who was a well-known London pewterer in the latter half of the eighteenth century. Others are marked " Boardman and Hart, N. York." I have seen quite a number of pieces—cups, mugs, and small pitchers—marked " Boardman," or " Boardman and Co., New York." The marks on their pieces have curious variations, some having, besides the name, a circle about the size of a ten-cent piece, inside of which is an eagle with spread wings grasping a sheaf of thunderbolts. In other cases the mark is an oval about the same size as the one previously spoken of, and in this is an eagle also, but with drooping wings, the most forlorn bird that ever was seen. Why the change?

Now, Timothy Boardman & Company were dealers in pewter and block tin at 178 Water Street, New York, in 1824. The firm was Boardman & Hart, at the same address, in 1828. By 1832 they had moved to 6 Burling Slip, and they were there until 1841, at which time the pewter was dropped from their business and they called themselves makers of Britannia Ware. In fact 1841 is the last year in which the trade of pewterer appears in the New York City Directory, and the trade gradually died out at about the same time all over the country.

Another interesting mark is Hamlin, New York;

this was prior to 1786. The touch is an eagle with spread wings, and over the eagle thirteen stars.

In New York in 1743 appeared the following advertisement:

"John Halden, braiser from London, near the old slip Market in New York, makes and sells all sorts of copper and brass kettles, tea kettles, coffee potts, pye pans, warming pans, and all sorts of copper and brass ware, also sells all sorts of hard metal and pewter wares."

The next year (1744) James Leddel, at the "Sign of the Platter," in Dock Street, sold pewter. In the end of this same year he moved to the end of Wall Street.

Robert Boyle, in 1745, called his shop the "Sign of the Gilt Dish," he had his shop in Dock Street too, William Bradford had his shop in Hanover Square.

In the first New York Directory, published in the year 1786, and which is about the size of an "Old Farmer's Almanac," the names of Francis Bassett, 218 Queen Street; Henry Will, 3 Water Street, and William Kirkby, 23 Dock Street, are the only ones of pewterers. In 1794 the trade of pewterer was for the first time combined with that of plumber, and Malcolm M'Ewen & Son, corner of Water Street and Beekman Slip, was the first firm to advertise it. William Kirkby, who was mentioned as one of the three pewterers who were put down in the first Directory, advertised in the "Mercury" that he would take old pewter or beeswax in exchange for new pewter or hard metal.

Among the early New England names of men who

Fig. 43. AMERICAN PEWTER. REED AND BARTON. EARLY NINETEENTH CENTURY

carried on the trade of pewterers were those of Richard Graves, who established himself in Salem, Mass., and Henry Shrimpton, of Boston, was a well-known pewter merchant.

Figure 41 is a piece of American pewter made by Homans & Co., Cincinnati. It is a pitcher seven and a half inches high, of a good grade of pewter and of good form, somewhat in the style of the old tankards, though the cover has a rising top, which is never seen on very early specimens; but it is interesting as being one of the rarely found American marked specimens.

In the early part of the nineteenth century there were silversmiths who practised the art of pewter-making as well. Reed & Barton, of New York, was such a firm, and they made much good ware of all the useful articles,—small pitchers, mugs, mustard-pots, etc. It is interesting to learn that this firm is reviving the making of pewter, using their old moulds for the purpose.

In England the manufacture of pewter has never wholly died, but it is confined to a few firms, one of the largest being Brown & Englefield, of London. Its ware embraces many kinds of moulds for jellies, jugs for hot water, pepper-pots, and plates.

I am frequently asked the prices of old pewter plates and dishes. It is hard to give any definite figures, for under the excitement of the auction-room larger prices are often given than can be commanded at private sale. Plates in good condition, 8, 9, 10, or 11 inches in diameter, should bring from $1.25 to $2.50 each. Larger-sized round plates and trenchers, 12, 14, or

16 inches in diameter, are worth from $3 to $6 apiece, while those measuring 20 inches and more are worth from $6 to $10. Embossed, and engraved, or wriggled-work pieces are worth considerably more.

Museums, as a rule, do not have their pewter cleaned, and this example is followed by most English collectors. If, however, you prefer yours bright, and you have found it in a bad condition, a good plan is to soak it in hot water in which a small quantity of potash (a piece as large as a hickory-nut to a quart of water) has been perfectly dissolved. The pewter can remain in the water a day or two without injury. Then rub the pieces very carefully with a cork dipped in oil and a little of the finest sand, and polish with a chamois-skin and whitening. Personally I do not indorse the use of the sand, but it is often employed. You can keep your pewter bright by washing it frequently in hot soap and water, and rubbing with whitening. This, of course, is after you have once got it polished up.

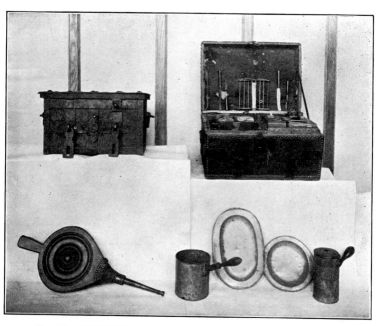

Fig. 44. GENERAL WASHINGTON'S STRONG BOX, MESS–
CHEST WITH PEWTER UTENSILS AND BELLOWS
National Museum, Washington, D. C.

PART III

BRASS WARE

PART III

BRASS WARE

It is not easy to decide just when the first use of brass, as we understand the term, began, or where. We read that a "brazen" bull was cast by Perillus, of Athens, for Phalaris, of Agrigentum, in 570 B.C. It was made hollow, to receive victims who were to be roasted, and the throat was so contrived as to make their groans seem like the bellowings of the animal. The artist was made its first victim (possibly so that he should not make such another work of art), and eventually the king himself was obliged to try it in his own person! This was in 549 B.C.

The term "brass" is frequently employed in the Scriptures from the time of Job down, yet there is nothing to indicate that it was the alloy with which we are familiar in modern times. In fact it seems that the first makers of brass as we know it were the Romans, for they made and used a compound which they called auricalchum, which seems to have possessed the properties of what we call brass. It was through the conquests of this people that its use and the knowledge of its composition was extended through Europe.

The earliest traces of its use in England are those

quaint mediæval monuments called "brasses," which are found over the tombs of civil and ecclesiastical dignitaries. These brasses, though none are represented in this book, are worthy a note just here, since they are the earliest form of brass extant. The oldest specimens date back to the first half of the thirteenth century, when they gradually displaced the tombs and effigies carved in stone, which had made such conspicuous features in the churches up to that time. The brasses were of Latten, or hard brass, and were frequently set into the pavement of the churches, thus taking up no room, and for that reason becoming very popular.

Although the value of the metal contributed to the wholesale destruction of these brasses, very many specimens are still found in England, and they were at one time common in France, Flanders and Germany. The Reign of Terror in France swept away the brasses as it did so many other valuable objects, but in Germany there may still be found instances which go back to the thirteenth century, such as that of the Bishop of Verdun (1231).

In England the best known of the thirteenth-century brasses is that of Sir Roger de Trumpington (1290), who went to Palestine with Prince Edward (afterward Edward I). He is represented as cross-legged, showing, so the theory is, that he had been to the Holy Land. Six or seven more such instances are known. Fourteenth-century brasses are more common, and in the sixteenth century the representations became portraits.

Fig. 45. ENGLISH BRASS KNOCKER Fig. 46. AMERICAN BRASS KNOCKER

Brasses cut in Flanders are by no means common in England, though they do occur, and they can be easily distinguished from those of English workmanship. The Flemish brasses had the figures engraved in the centre of a large plate, the background being filled in with a scroll or diapered work. The English figures, on the other hand, were cut in outline, and set into a corresponding depression in the stone. A few Flemish-made cut brasses are known, but their work was more florid in design, the lines were shallower, and they were cut with a chisel-pointed tool instead of a burin.

There is a certain class of brasses known as " palimpsests,"—old brasses which have been taken out of their original settings, re-engraved on the back, and made to do duty for a second person. Thus a brass commemorative of Margaret Bulstrode (1540), on being removed from its position, was discovered to have been made originally for Thomas Totyngton, abbot of St. Edmund's Bury, in 1312. The abbey was surrendered to Henry VIII in 1539, so within the year the work of spoliation had begun, and the abbot's brass had been done over to serve for Mistress Bulstrode. One reason for the wholesale stealing of these old brasses, and their re-erection when newly engraved on the back, was on account of the difficulty of getting sheet brass in England. All that was used prior to 1650 was of Continental make.

To preserve the remainder of these interesting and valuable records, from which many a family record has been perfected, several societies have grown up in Great Britain, the most active being that of the city of Cambridge, which boasts a large membership. There are on record over 4,000 of these brasses in churches and cathedrals, and it is expected that soon all that remain will be recorded and kept in repair. There are many antiquarians who make collections of rubbings from the brasses, as the inscriptions are universally quaint, and this is the only way that a proof, so to speak, can be obtained, so that the engraving of the devices and lettering shows up.

There is one of these brasses at the church at Stratford-on-Avon, to view which so many Americans repair, and the wording on it has been copied many times, although in places it is much worn away by the feet of pilgrims to that shrine. It runs thus:

> " GOOD FREND FOR IESVS SAKE FORBEARE,
> TO DIGG THE DVST ENCLOASED HEARE:
> BLESE BE YE MAN YT SPARES THES STONES,
> AND CVRST BE HE YT MOVES MY BONES."

Underneath it lies the tomb of William Shakespeare.

Although the metal of which many of the brasses were made came from Germany, which country was famous for her production of brass during the Middle Ages, it was made in England in increasing quantities. During the reign of Henry VIII, an act of Parliament was passed, prohibiting the export of brass, showing that not enough was made for home consumption. A curious detail of this enactment is that it was not repealed till so lately as 1799. During the reign of Queen Elizabeth the manufacture of brass was much

Fig. 47. FIREPLACE AND FENDER
Langdon House, Portsmouth House, N. H.

Fig. 48. FIREPLACE AND ANDIRONS. ENGLAND, COLONIAL
HOUSE

developed and encouraged, and a patent for the working of calamine stone was granted by the Queen to William Humfrey and Christopher Schutz, securing to them the exclusive right to manufacture brass. The patent rights issued to these men was gradually extended, and finally became vested in a company called "The Governors, Assistants, and Societies of the City of London of and for the Mineral and Battery Works,"—a long and far from clear designation. This company, however, continued to exercise its functions down to the year 1710, when it was dissolved.

During the Middle Ages the ordinary domestic pin, which has long been an article of feminine economy, was made of brass. In the fifteenth century it had become of so much importance as an article of commerce in England, that in 1483 the importation of pins was forbidden by statute. Only the best pins were made of brass, for there were inferior ones made of iron wire blanched, and it was against these that the enactment was directed. By 1636 the Pinmakers of London formed a corporation, and the manufacture was subsequently removed to Bristol and Birmingham, the latter town becoming the principal centre for the industry. Brass works or foundries had been started in Bristol in 1702, and by a man named Turner, in Birmingham, about 1740.

The early settlers in America were dependent on London for their pins and needles, and there are few lists sent over by them which did not include an order for one or the other of these articles. They were not sold as now, by the paper, but by the hundred.

In 1761 Colonel George Washington sent to London for some articles for his own wardrobe, and for those of Mrs. Washington and Nelly Custis. Mrs. Washington's order was for—

—"a salmon-coloured tabby velvet with satin flowers; ruffles of Brussels lace or point, to cost twenty pounds; fine silk hose, white and black satin shoes; six pairs of mitts; six pairs of best kid gloves; one dozen of most fashionable handkerchiefs; one dozen knots and breast-knots; real minikin [very small] pins and hair pins; a puckered petticoat, six pounds of perfumed powder; handsome breast flowers; and some sugar candy."

In the same order were enumerated these articles for "Miss Custis, aged six."

"A coat of fashionable silk with bib-apron, ruffles and lace tucker; four fashionable dresses of long lawn; fine cambric frocks; a satin capuchin hat and neckatees; satin shoes and white kid gloves; silver shoe buckles, sleeve buttons, aigrettes and six thousand pins, large, short and minikin; a fashionable doll to cost a guinea; gingerbread; toys, comfits and sugar images."

One would think that the gingerbread would have been a trifle stale when it reached Mount Vernon!

So necessary were pins that it was not long before the colonists appreciated the benefit to accrue to them by their manufacture, and the people of the Carolinas were stimulated by the offers of prizes for the first-made pins and needles. This was by 1775. At a later day than this several pin-making machines were invented in the United States, and during the war of 1812 the price of pins rose to such an extent that the manufacture was actually started, but it was not par-

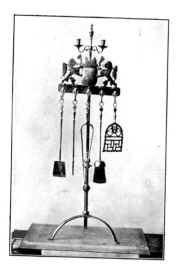

Fig. 49. BRASS FIRE-SET
Collection of Mr. Lattimore

Fig. 50. OLD BRASS ANDIRONS
From the Collection of A. Killgore, Esq.

ticularly successful until 1836. By 1824, however, Mr. Lemuel Wright, of Massachusetts, had patented a pin-making machine in England, which established the industry on its present basis.

Various processes are employed in the making of brass. It may be cast, rolled in sheets, or drawn into wire. It was not until 1781 that James Emerson patented the direct production of brass from copper and zinc, and his method gradually displaced the old or calamine process. Some of the most important factors in the development of the brass trade have been the introduction of rolling-mills in the early part of the last century, and the application of stamp and die in 1769.

All brass is now made by melting together copper and zinc, but the term " cast brass " is applied when the article receives its form from a mould, and is not afterward rolled, drawn, hammered, or spun. For this purpose the charge is melted in small furnaces heated by coke. The moulds for the casting of brass are commonly of sand, and when the cast object is still warm it is dipped into water, which detaches most of the sand, and it is then dressed, ground, and burnished. The proportion of copper in brass varies from 66 to 75 per cent. In the latter proportion is made the best English brass.

For sheet brass the metal is first cast in bars, or what are known as " strips," and these strips are pressed cold through rollers. When they are sufficiently thin, to prevent cracking, the metal is annealed at a red heat, and the surface is cleaned of oxide by immersion in diluted sulphuric acid. These processes are repeated until the sheet is of proper size and thickness.

" Red metal " and " Prince's metal " are two varieties, the former being used in the button trade. Birmingham, England, originally famous for its iron work, acquired a reputation for brass buttons. Gold lace had long been conspicuous for ornamenting riding-dresses, and, as it grew old-fashioned, its place was taken by brass buttons. The eighteenth and the first part of the nineteenth centuries may be called "the brass-button era." What steel has been to Sheffield and cotton to Manchester, has brass been to Birmingham, and brass-founding and brass-making are among its peculiar industries.

Of all English centres of industry, Birmingham is perhaps the most remarkable for the variety of its products. In fact its boast is that it is never badly off, since it has so many strings to its bow. Nothing is too hot or too heavy, too minute or too great, for Birmingham to attempt, and among the multitudinous objects manufactured there are heathen gods, umbrellas, matches and stained-glass windows, sewing-machines, brass beds, teapots and guns, roasting-jacks and swords, needles and buttons, fish-hooks and railroad cars.

Many of the good brass articles found in this country originated in Birmingham, and it is a pity that the workers in brass did not follow the example of the pewterers, and stamp their ware. Only a very few pieces are known which are marked in any way, and one of them is a very ornamental door-lock of fine

Fig. 51. BRASS AND COPPER BRAZIER
From the Collection of Mr. George Brodhead

Fig. 52. SPANISH BRASERO AND BOWLS
From the Collection of Mrs. Charles P. Barry

workmanship. It is now to be seen in the South Kensington Museum, and has scratched upon it, "Richard Bickford, Londini, fecit 1675." But centuries before this knockers were made of brass, as times grew more peaceful, and the coming guest no longer wound his horn or rapped with his sword to announce his arrival. The most famous of the ancient knockers which now remain in England is at Oxford, and has quite a long and unusual history.

Brasenose College, Oxford, was so called on account of this knocker, which was on the outer door of Brasenose Hall. In 1334 the Oxford students migrated to the town of Stamford, owing to a riotous feud, and took with them their knocker, which was a brass head, and was the emblem of their college society. At the Lincolnshire town they built a new Brasenose Hall, and fastened thereon the nose of brass. After a time the breach was healed, and the students returned to Oxford, the building they had used passing into the hands of the corporation of Stamford. In 1688 the building was torn down, save only the ancient doorway. A house was built on the site, which went into private hands, together with the doorway, door, and knocker. At a recent sale of this property (1890) Brasenose College became the purchaser, and has recovered and restored to Oxford, after a lapse of five and a half centuries, the knocker wrenched off by the departing students of the fourteenth century.

This knocker, or "nose" is in the form of a lion's head with an iron ring through the mouth. The brows of the lion are very prominent, and the teeth are rudely engraved, though the head is well modelled. The nose is by no means so prominent as to justify the name. This pattern has long been a favourite one in England, and in Figure 45 is given a good example of it. This is an old knocker, and for many years was both ornamental and useful on a hospitable door in New England. By the last quarter of the eighteenth century the eagle began to be more esteemed among us than the lion, even though he was the king of beasts, and some brass-worker—a sturdy American patriot, let us hope—devised for Colonial doorways a bird with fierce aspect and spread wings. One of these is shown in Figure 46. It is many years old, and, like the lion, served in New England, for many a long year, to announce the coming guest.

Once within the house, two important necessities were heat and light. The former was supplied largely by great fireplaces, and in many of these were to be found brass fenders, fire-dogs, and fire-tongs, shovels, etc. These were often very handsome and quite costly affairs, and most of them were brought from England, at least in the early days. The brass fenders are not often found now, but one is shown in Figure 47, which is in a room in the old Langdon House, at Portsmouth, New Hampshire. In passing I would call attention to the superb carving of the over-mantel, of the mantel itself, and all about the room. This famous old house was built by John Langdon in 1784. He was an earnest and devoted patriot, and was five times chosen governor of New Hampshire. He made a famous

Fig. 53. KITCHEN OF THE WHIPPLE HOUSE AT IPSWICH, MASS.

Fig. 54. BRASS CANDLESTICKS RUSSIAN

Fig. 55. BRASS CANDLESTICKS RUSSIAN

speech in 1777, which shows of what stuff these American gentlemen were made. He said:

"I have a thousand dollars in hard money; I will pledge my plate for three thousand more; I have seventy hogsheads of Tobago rum, which will be sold for the most that they will bring. They are at the service of the State. If we succeed in defending our homes and firesides, I may be remunerated; if we do not, then the property will be of no value to me."

Before this very handsome fireplace General Washington has stood when he visited Portsmouth in 1789, and he has recorded it as the handsomest house in the town. Louis Philippe and his brothers were entertained here, and so was President Monroe. They nearly all leave records of the beauty and elegance of the mansion, and one of the guests, the Marquis de Chastellux, wrote in 1782,—

After dinner we went to drink tea with Mr. Langdon. He is a handsome man and of noble carriage. His house is elegant and well furnished, and the apartments well wainscotted."

Indeed in these old houses the fireplace was the centre of the home, so to speak, for in many of the Colonial houses the rooms were large and stately, and to keep the blood from almost congealing, it was necessary to gather pretty closely to the fire. As befitted its importance, the fireplace was handsomely wainscotted, and in Figure 48 there is a type of woodwork surrounding the generous hearth which is earlier than that shown in Figure 47. In it is a pair of nice old fire-dogs,— "rights and lefts" they were called when they had a curve back of the brass dog, and about where the iron foot joined on. When half-grown trees, sawed into logs three or four feet long, were piled up in such a fireplace as this, you can imagine that a great heat was sent out into the room. The fire demanded much attention, and for this purpose handsome fire-sets were both made here and imported. Such a set is shown in Figure 49, though this one is more ornamental than is common. In humble homes the housewife was satisfied if she had a curved arm screwed into the woodwork of the mantel, and in this rested the shovel and tongs. Often a piece of marble scored in squares stood neatly in the corner of the hearth, and the fire-irons were set into the scores to keep them from slipping. I have seen several ornamental sets like the one in Figure 49, and one or two which were made in this country and had the foot and upright made of iron or steel instead of brass. This one came from an old manor house in England, where it had been in use for scores of years. The openwork shovel was to take up hot coals for putting into warming-pans or braziers, or for the necessary foot-warmer to be used on Sunday.

I have said that some of these articles were made in this country, but just how early brass was made here it would be hard to say. Probably in a small way it was commenced early, for braziers were among the early comers. During the first anxious days in 1620, when the able-bodied men were exploring the coast of Plymouth harbour near where the " Mayflower " lay at anchor, in order to choose a good place for the settlement, they had a sharp encounter with the Nauset

Fig. 56. BRASS CANDLESTICK, RUSSIAN
From the Collection of Mrs. Charles P. Barry

Fig. 57. BRASS UTENSILS
From the Collection of Mr. Wilford R. Lawshe

Indians. After the victory, when the Pilgrims came together again, they picked up eighteen arrows. Some of these were tipped with brass, some with deer-horn, and some with the claws of eagles. It is now supposed that this brass came from the wreck of a French vessel in 1616, for these first foes of the Pilgrims were the Nausets, the only tribe between Chatham and Provincetown.

During the next century many braziers came from England and settled in various parts of the country. The first New York directory, published in 1786, gives the names of James Kip, Brass Founder, 59 Broadway, and Abram Montayne, at 13 King Street. The ironmongers and tinplaters, no doubt, also sold brass ware, and brass hinges and handles were sold to the furniture-makers before we made them here.

Various brass works were established in different parts of the country, and the Michauds, father and son, who travelled here extensively from 1793-1796, and again in 1802, tell in their "Early Western Travels," of finding in the southwestern part of Pennsylvania, "about two miles from Liberty Town, Probes' Furnace, a foundry established by a Frenchman from Alsace." He made all kinds of brass vessels, and also worked in copper. The largest brass kettles he made were capable of holding about 200 pints. These were sent to Kentucky and "Tennessea," where they were used in the preparation of salt by evaporation. The smaller-sized kettles were for household use. The son, Francois, states also, that for the most part the inhabitants of Lancaster, Pennsylvania, are "armourers, hatters, saddlers, and coopers, the armourers of Lancaster having long been celebrated for their manufacture of rifle-barrelled guns."

In Colonial accoutrements much brass was used, many eagles being cut from sheet brass and put on belts and haversacks. I have in mind now two such eagles, of different sizes, which have been brought from seclusion by a "Colonial Dame," and mounted on two small panels on her staircase. Michaud the younger also says:

"At Springfield, or near it, is Mays-lick, where there is a salt-mine. For evaporation, they make use of brazen pots containing about 200 pints and similar in form to those used in France for making lye. They put ten or twelve in a row in a pit four feet deep, and at the ends throw in billets of wood and kindle a fire. These sort of kilns consume great amounts of wood."

In Figure 50 are shown several styles of old andirons, all of which are reproduced for use to-day. The wedding outfit of Judith Sewall, daughter of Judge Samuel Sewall, who kept the voluminous diary which is such a mine of wealth as to customs and manners in New England during the last part of the seventeenth and first part of the eighteenth centuries, is often quoted as showing what was demanded as necessary by a well-to-do bride of that period. The list of her brass ware is given in full, with the prices which it was deemed proper to pay for it, and I give it here so as to show what an important part this metal played in domestic utensils two hundred years ago. After specifying the furniture for a "chamber," the list proceeds:

Fig. 58. BRASS COOKING-UTENSILS AND CANDLESTICKS
In Deerfield Memorial Hall

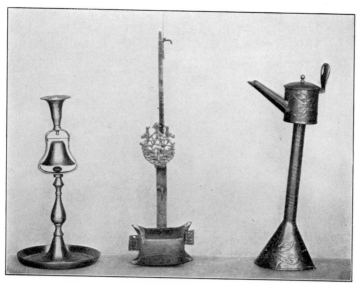

Fig. 59. BRASS CANDLESTICK AND LAMPS
From the Collections of Mr. George Brodhead and Mrs. E. Wetmore

One bell-metal Skillet of 2 quarts, one ditto one Quart.

One good large warming-pan and cover fit for an iron handle.

4 Pair of strong Iron Dogs with brass heads about five or six shillings a pair.

A Brass Hearth for a chamber with Dogs, Shovels, Tongs, and Fender of the Newest Fashion (the fire is to ly on Iron.)

A strong Brass Mortar That will hold about a Quart with a Pestle.

Two pair of large Brass sliding Candlesticks about four shillings a Pair.

Two pair of large Brass Candlesticks not sliding of the Newest Fashion about five or six shillings a Pair.

Four Brass snuffers with stands.

Six small Brass Chafing-dishes about four shillings apiece.

One Brass basting Ladle; one larger Brass Ladle.

One Pair Chamber Bellows with Brass noses.

One small hair broom sutable to the Bellows.

Before the days of fireplaces and chimneys (the latter were not in use till about the middle of the fourteenth century), hot coals were carried about from room to room, and placed in metal pans near at hand, so that the occupants might find the chill a little mitigated. Such receptacles were made of brass or copper, and remained in use for some hundreds of years. Fashions and comforts spread slowly in those days, and what had long been obsolete in London might have become the "proper thing" in the country districts. Sometimes these receptacles for hot coals had little holes in them; in other cases the metal itself, becoming heated, gave out warmth in that way. Such a warmer is seen in Figure 51, and a very aristocratic one it is, with the lower half of brass with copper ornaments rivetted on, and the upper half copper with brass ornaments on it. The bail is of iron. It is a splendid piece, all beaten work, the rivets showing quite plainly even in the photograph. It has a copper bottom and stands on three brass feet. The lion would seem to reveal its English origin, though it was bought from a Russian Jew who had brought it from his own country. It shows evidence of much use, and the inside is scarred and scorched with the coals which have been put in it.

Under the general heading of " heat " it may be well to notice the various styles of braziers which were also in common use. These braziers were open pans for burning wood or charcoal. The old Roman brazier was a bronze tripod with a round dish above the fire, and a vase below for perfumes. It occupied the *atrium,* and represented the abode of hospitality and sanctuary, even after the process of cooking had been banished to another apartment. The smoke was of course unpleasant, and in order to prevent this the bark was peeled from wood, the wood long soaked in water, then dried, and anointed with oil. The Greeks sought to mitigate the " smoke nuisance " by burning costly and perfumed gums, and spices, and scented woods.

In Figure 52 is an antique Spanish *brasero,* with solid and heavy handles by which to carry it, and around the rim is an engraved border. The legs are rivetted on, and each terminates in a small foot. On either hand are brass vessels, the one with the foot for serving, and the bowl for either cooking or serving.

The Japanese warming-apparatus is similar to the Spanish *brasero,* and is used with a handful of coals, but it is so inefficient that in midwinter, particularly

Fig. 60. PAIR OF BRASS LAMPS
From the Collection of Mr. William M. Hoyt

Fig. 61. TALL BRASS LAMP
From the Collection of Mr. William M. Hoyt

in the northern part of the kingdom, the people depend principally on their clothes for warmth, piling on gown after gown, and then topping these with splendid furs.

In Judith Sewall's brass ware were mentioned ladles of various sizes, to be used in cooking, and in Figure 53 quite a collection of these utensils are shown hanging in the kitchen of the Whipple House at Ipswich, Mass., in company with many other articles, the uses of which have been rendered obsolete by the introduction of modern methods. In the fireplace, tradition says, a calf could be roasted whole, and when you see the extent of its dusky recesses, you can well believe the tale.

When we consider the insufficient and wholly inadequate methods of obtaining light, we are surprised that our ancestors had any eyes at all. William Wood, in his "New England's Prospect" (1634), says:

"Out of the Pines is gotten candlewood that is so much spoke of, which may serve as a shift among poore folks, but I cannot commend it for Singular good because it is something sluttish, dropping a pitchy kind of substance where it stands."

But this was very early in the country's history, by 1635 they were better off for lights.

Candlesticks of many types and from many countries, both for religious and secular uses, are shown in Figures 54, 55, 56, and 57, all of them being of brass. A number of them are of Jewish origin, for the Jews have always been celebrated for their skill in metal work. In Bible days at Tyre and Sidon "they traded in vessels of brass in thy market." The large branched candlestick in Figure 55 is for religious use, as are the three in Figure 56, the low one on the right hand having places for candles for each day in the week, while the one on the left with the two birds is a Chinese stick, for use in a temple. While it is true that the ordinary so-called " Chinese curio " often has had no real connection with the Flowery Kingdom, once in a while a real export from the land of rice and Boxers appears to delight the soul of the collector. A Chinese brass lock came to hand the other day, hand-made, of course, and fashioned to fasten together two staples in the manner of a padlock. With it went two keys, one to lock it by pushing back a spring inside, the other to release the spring. This latter was a most elaborate affair, notched and split in intricate ways, intended no doubt to foil the cupidity of the cleverest of Celestial burglars. The Chinese love to make many of their curious ornaments just verging on the grotesque, like this candlestick. The one next to the Chinese stick is Portuguese, this nation also excelling in metal work at an early period, although they devoted themselves chiefly to silverware.

More common types of candlesticks are seen in Figure 57, the little ones being for bedroom use, while the tall one would grace the dining-table, or help to light the card-table when neighbours dropped in for a social game. The strange-looking object on the right hand of the picture is a spoon-mould, and in it were run many dozens of pewter spoons, like one of those shown in Part I. Behind the mould is a brass dipper, and in the rear is a long-handled spoon for use in a big pot. The smoothing-iron is of brass, and has

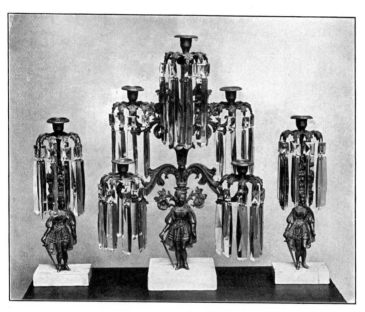

Fig. 62. GIRANDOLES
Collection of Mr. William M. Hoyt

a small drawer which pulls out, and was filled with hot coals when in use. The graceful goblet is not a common article, although more vessels were made of this metal than we would deem pleasant or sanitary now.

Various forms of candlesticks are to be noted in Figure 58, the one with the little knob on the stem being one of the "sliding candlesticks" which Judith Sewall desired. The lamp is also a good article, and is intended either to be carried in the hand, or to be hung on the wall by means of the ring which is visible on its edge opposite the handle. There were brass lamps and pewter ones as well which were made at an early period for burning camphine, a volatile and inflammable form of spirits of turpentine, obtained from the pine-trees which were so abundant in the Southern States. It burned with a very white light, and, even though dangerous, was much used.

A brass snuffers and tray for use with candles is also shown in this illustration, as well as some skillets with the tripods on which they stood among the ashes, in order to get the necessary heat for cooking. Frying-pans also were often of this metal, and one with a wooden handle is seen in the background. It was one of the housekeeper's most cherished ornaments of the kitchen, as it hung on the wall polished to a mirror-like brightness.

Brass articles, whatever their use, were hard to procure, and were expected to last long and be handed down from one generation to another. It is almost pathetic to see how scant the household goods were. Things that we would not think worthy of mention were specified with the greatest particularity in inventories and wills.

One Edward Thatcher, of Pirton, England, died May 10, 1595. He left what was considered a large estate, and among the articles enumerated are, " to my grandson one fallowe Cowe and best bed and one greate Brasse Candlesticke." To another grandson he leaves "one browne Cowe short horned Coverlett and a paire of sheets next best." To yet another, "one fallowe heifer with bed and payer of sheets of the third sorte and one Brasse Candlesticke." He was evidently attached to his daughter-in-law, for he says, "To daughter in Lawe Ellynor Marshe a white Couerlett payer of blanketts, platter, pottinger, little Caudron, her mother's Weddinge Ringe and her best partlett, she to take her share quietly and without troubling my Exor." Let us hope that Ellynor and her mother-in-law had hair of the same shade, otherwise what could she have done with the "best partlett"?

Richard Prowst, of Imscott, in Hartland, England, died Sept. 2, 1580, leaving the following bequest: "To Joane my daughter, my grete brazen panne wth certaine ffethers that lyeth in a barrell in my house."

In 1598, in Norfolk, England, a man named Fuller leaves to his wife Ann, "all the household stuffe she brought me, such as brasse, pewter, bedding, fowles, etc., at her death to go to Thomas Fuller the younger." These same people, by the way, had two sons named Thomas and two named William, which might, it

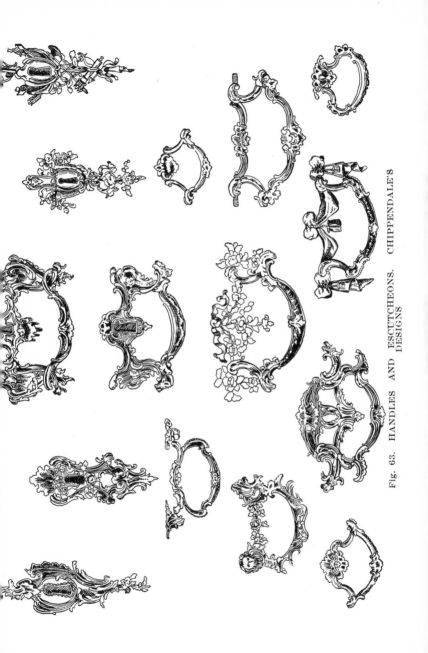

Fig. 63. HANDLES AND ESCUTCHEONS. CHIPPENDALE'S DESIGNS

would seem, have caused endless confusion in the family.

Now, if we cross the water to America and come down nearly a century later, we find that brass household articles are still highly considered. In "A true Inventory of the Personal Estate of Capt. John Sanford who Deceased the 25th of January, 1687, Taken by us Whose hands are hereunto subscribed and valued According to New England money," are mentioned the following household articles:

	£	s.	d.
"Imprimis. Wearing cloathes	1	08	00
Item. Beds bedsteads and furniture thereunto belonging	8	10	00
Item. Brasse Weare	1	00	00."

His table and stools are also mentioned as being worth one pound.

The inventory of Governor Bradford, dated 1657, has already been given in the section on Pewter, and it is to be seen that he valued his "Kittles" and candlesticks very highly. Captain Miles Standish had three brass kettles, four iron pots, one skillet, and one warming-pan, the bulk of his estate being in books and livestock.

It seems strange that brass lamps were not more often mentioned, for they were by no means uncommon and were of various types. The simplest and most primitive were called "Betty lamps," and were small trays into which some grease was put with a bit of twisted rag in the centre, which, when burning, gave a feeble ray. These lamps generally had long handles by which they were hung on the wall, and they were long in use both in this country and in England, and not alone in the cottage districts either. They were called "cruiseys" and "kials" as well as "Bettys," and in Figure 59 are shown two lamps and one candlestick. The central lamp, though this specimen was brought from Damascus, is similar to the Betty lamp, although the latter was made to burn only one wick, while this is made for four, one at each corner. Much brass work, both old and new, comes from Damascus,—there are countless trays, some of them on feet and intended to hold coffee sets; there are bowls, and lamps, and pitchers, or flagons. Women and children are employed to restamp patterns on old trays from which the design has been worn by constant use, but to men only is entrusted the work of making new ones. Since the attention of collectors has been turned to brass ware, the shores of the Mediterranean, Syria, North Africa, and the shores of the Adriatic, as well as Spain, have been scoured for rare and antique specimens. The most elaborate and beautiful work comes from Persia, the lace-like design and the chasing on the thick brass being equally admirable. Some of the fine old pieces are dated, which of course adds to their value.

The brass alms-dish of the dervish is his most treasured possession, and was often made in the shape of the black seed of the Seychelles palm, and exquisitely decorated. Fine braziers are also to be found in Persia, but many of them are the newest of the new, successfully "treated." Shaving-basins of brass are

Fig. 64. HANDLES AND ESCUTCHEONS FROM 1750 TO 1800

found in many countries, with a curved indentation of the rim for the throat to fit into. Travellers to-day are often amused to see a barber pursuing his vocation by the roadside, the customer holding the basin under his chin while the barber works.

In looking once more at Figure 59 the old brass lamp seems quaint enough. It is made from sheet brass, and is ornamented with a punched design. These lamps were made either to stand, or to hang by means of the device seen on the body of the lamp. The long wick gave but a feeble flicker, and smoked beside. Yet such things as this were used for the only luminary of a family for an evening, when their entire energies were devoted to making it burn and keeping the wick at a proper distance out of the oil. No wonder that our ancestors invented that old saw, " Early to bed and early to rise! "

The third object in the picture is a cast brass candlestick of unusual design. The central portion is a bell which swings slightly to and fro and gives a pleasing note when struck. It is possible that this was used for a table light or at an inn, where the bell became useful in summoning an attendant. I have seen only two pairs like this, and both came from New England.

When I look at these candlesticks I often think of an experience I once had in the lovely old cathedral city of York, England. When I went there I carried letters of introduction to one of the old families, whose ancestor some one or two generations back had married an American girl, some time before the so-called

" American Invasion." They had a house, built into the walls of the city, which stood on ground once belonging to the cathedral, and which had been in possession of the family about six hundred years. Of course we were anxious to see the house, and sent our letters. Members of the family came to call, but we were out, and then they sent us an invitation to dine. This we accepted, mentioning, in the note, that we begged to be excused for not appearing in evening gowns, as we were travelling, and had left most of our baggage in London. The messenger returned with a note in which the invitation was changed from dinner to lunch! If that house had not been six hundred years old we would not have taken the second cut, but interest dominated pride and we went. On the walls of the great hall in which we were received were suits of armour and numerous brass plates inscribed with the names of the kings, queens, and princelings who had visited the place. The host, who held the position of High Sheriff, and whose ancestors for many generations back had held the same office, was attired in small-clothes and a wig, as he had just been officiating at service in the minster, in attendance on some dignitaries of the city. When we went into the dining-hall,—and " hall " it was truly, with a clerestory with small stained-glass windows through which the light filtered softly down, and in which the dining-table seemed like an oasis, so large was the apartment,—I noticed beside the host's chair a huge brass gong hung on a standard. On this he struck when he wanted the butler or any of the numerous footmen who were in

Fig. 65. PIPKINS AND FENDERS
The Fenders are Chippendale's Designs; the Pipkins of the same Period

attendance. The stick which he used for this purpose was laid beside his plate. My curiosity getting the better of me, he told me that the gong had been in use some hundreds of years by his forebears, and that the old custom was retained by him. When I look on these candlesticks I wonder if some old Englishman in a more humble walk of life smote on the bell when he wanted Betty to come and take away the roast beef and Yorkshire pudding, and bring his pipe and grog, and light the candles with a hot coal from the fireplace!

The tall arms from which the fire utensils hung were also generally provided with two or more places for candles, showing that the popular seat was within reach of both fire and light.

Sea coal was introduced about 1744, and at the same time " Pennsylvania fireplaces" came into use, Benjamin Franklin having invented his grate shortly before. Steel hearths and stove-grates could be bought here by 1751, and iron stoves with feet and handles of brass were also in use. Lamps came in pairs, and were frequently made of cast brass, like those in Figure 60. These were for burning sperm oil and had double wicks, and though by no means givers of much light they were vastly better than candles. It is not common to find a pair,—indeed they are almost as unusual as a pair of china pitchers,—though many of these were sent over here for a period of eighty years or more. Now a single pitcher of one pattern is all we think of buying. This pair of lamps sold for fifteen dollars, but if you owned a pair you probably could not get half that amount for them,—and rightly too, for the dealer has his profit to make.

Very elegant lamps were sent over here for sale, both from England and France, and I show one in Figure 61. In most cases they were made of bronze or brass water-gilt. Such lamps as these were often ornamented with a row of glass prisms hanging from the shade, and sometimes girandoles and sconces for the wall, holding candles, were of this same material. Very elegant ones were sent here from France, having as a centre ornament a china plaque beautifully decorated either with a head or with figures *à la* Watteau, and such were choice parlour ornaments.

The " best room," " south parlour," or " drawing-room,"—no matter what it was called by the stately lady who presided over it,—was never considered complete unless it had on the mantle-shelf a set of candelabra or girandoles with prisms, or " lustres," as they were called. Three candles in the middle one and two each in the side ones were deemed the proper pattern, and very ornamental they were, although they have been banished to the attic for some decades. Now we are beginning to haul them forth again, and have to hunt about to find the prisms, for these are often fewer than they should be, owing to the depredations of the children, who love to watch the play of colours as they filter through the sparkling glass. A quaint pair with room for more than the usual number of candles is seen in Figure 62.

Even the great makers of furniture, Chippendale, Sheraton, Hepplewhite, Adam Brothers, and Hope

Fig. 66. GEORGE WASHINGTON'S HALL LANTERN
In the National Museum, Washington

Fig. 67. BRASS CHANDELIER
St. Michael's Church, Charleston, S. C.

himself, did not consider it beneath their dignity to design fenders, girandoles, escutcheons and handles for furniture. When once you begin on the subject of metal mounts, which were chiefly of brass, you open the doors to a subject so vast that it would take a whole book to cover it properly. I have had many requests for light on this subject, as many people are anxious to restore to their furniture the handles and keyholes which properly belong to them, so I have had copied from the books of Chippendale, Hepplewhite and Sheraton some pages of designs showing these mounts. They even drew patterns for " pipkins " (scuttles) of copper and brass (as shown in Figure 65), and their wine-coolers were often bound with bands of these metals, sometimes handsomely wrought.

These fenders were usually made from sheet brass, cut into the desired patterns. When small ornaments and mounts were cast, the moulds were of wood. The Dutch as well as the English and French made handsome mounts, though the rage for these additions to furniture never reached such proportions in any other country as in France, and no maker ever gained the proficiency and skill in using them of Riesener, who began to make his elegant pieces during the period of Louis XV, but who is better known by his straight-legged pieces which have come to be called " Louis XVI style."

Every house with any pretensions to " gentility," or even comfort, had in the entrance-hall a lantern, either square or round, mounted in brass, and holding either a candle or a small lamp. The lantern in Figure 66 belonged to General and Mrs. Washington and hung in the hall at Mount Vernon. It has some handsome brass work on it. It was probably imported from England with most of the other household goods, and is now in the National Museum at Washington, where so many interesting relics of the Father of his Country are to be found. These lanterns hung from the ceiling by either chains or what were called " lines and tossels." Joseph Cox was a fashionable upholsterer from London, who had as his sign, " The Royal Bed." He was first in Dock Street and then in Wall Street, New York, and in 1773 had for sale "lines and a few very handsome balance tossels for hall lanthorns." He had also fire-screens and " voiders " (crumb-trays), both of brass.

All public buildings were lighted in the same primitive way as were private houses, and in most cases candles were the means used. Churches had large chandeliers of brass or bronze, and the one shown in Figure 67 still hangs in Saint Michael's Church, Charleston, S. C. It was made by G. Penton, a well-known maker in London, and was imported in 1803. It had holders for forty-five candles, and hung by a chain. It has recently been bronzed and fitted for gas, (1879), but still preserves its old look. It was quite a business to light all those candles and keep them snuffed, and the office of sexton was no sinecure. In this church there is a fine brass dove which forms a balance for the cover of the font when it is raised and in use. This also was of English make.

Many domestic utensils were of brass, not only tea-

Fig. 68. BRASS KETTLES AND PITCHER
From the Collection of Mr. George Brodhead

Fig. 69. MILK-CAN AND COOKING-UTENSILS
In the Mechanics Institute, Rochester, N. Y.

kettles, but jugs, sugar-bowls, and small pitchers as well. In Figure 68 are presented two kettles and a pitcher. The kettle with the coat of arms on it is of a pattern seldom seen, and has been much used. When it was new it had a wooden handle, but this has all been burned away, leaving only the iron pin which went through its centre. The other kettle is older yet, a battered veteran, made of hammered sheet brass and having a brass handle. I hope the pitcher was used only for hot water as a shaving jug, for I cannot conceive of drinking milk or any other fluid which had stood in such a receptacle.

Our ancestors generally, however, were not very particular on this point, and to-day in Holland the favourite milk-cans are of brass, similar to the one shown in Figure 69, which is a nice old Dutch piece, long in use. As usual it is of hammered brass, and seems a finer quality of metal than any of the other pieces, except the little perforated stand with feet. This stand is a beauty. It is made from a single piece of brass perforated in a pretty pattern, and once used to stand among the hot ashes to hold some object which was not suitable to be exposed to their heat. Perhaps the best "chaney" teapot was kept warm in this when company came of an afternoon, or the baby's milk was heated in it, in a little pipkin or an earthen mug. We shall never know just how useful it was; but it was often used, that is certain, for the feet, which were wooden knobs with iron pins through them, are all burned away, and the bottom shows frequent contact with hot coals. The teakettle in the same picture is a graceful one, and the two dishes in the same illustration were used for cooking or heating, after the food had been once thoroughly cooked in the great iron pot which hung in every fireplace.

There was another object in brass made by the Dutch which far exceeded the milk-can in usefulness, but in size is quite at the other end of the scale. This is the thimble. These articles were invented by a Dutchman or a Dutchwoman—and first brought to England in 1695. Thimbles were then worn on the thumb, and were called thumb-bells—after this thumbles, then thimbles, a very easy and natural transition.

The early thimbles were made of brass or iron, but a more luxurious age demanded them of gold, silver, horn, glass, or even of mother-of-pearl. You will find the latter in the Flowery Kingdom, where the little brown ladies use them in making their matchless embroideries, these tiny articles having a top and rim of gold, both metal and pearl-shell being exquisitely carved. Paul Revere, of Lexington fame, was noted for his handsome silver and gold thimbles and gold beads, as well as for the larger pieces of silver, copper, and brass ware which he made.

Handsome brass boxes were made in England, in Flanders, and America, with either raised or engraved decoration on them. They were used to hold tobacco, snuff, or small articles, sometimes served as money-boxes, or were hung at the church door to receive offerings. The word "tip" originated in the old coffee-houses, which were so popular in London. At the door was a brass box with a slit in it. Engraved on

Fig. 70. BRASS KETTLES
From the Collection of Mr. William M. Hoyt

Fig. 71. SUGAR BOWL AND PITCHER
From the Collection of Mr. George Brodhead

the top were the letters " T. I. P.," an abbreviation for the words, "To insure promptness." As customers departed they dropped into the box a small coin for the benefit of the waiters.

More precious to the housekeeper than little dishes and boxes and pitchers and pans were the great brass kettles, which were her pride and delight, even though it did require such a world of care to keep them polished to a proper state of brightness. Three sizes are shown in Figure 70, all of them in good condition. Since this picture was taken two of them have been sold for five dollars each. But there is another side to this picture, and if you are in luck you can find them for less. Within a few weeks I have seen three about the size of these, which were bought at a junk-shop in western New York. When the antique-lover saw one of them in the window, she went in, and, pursuing the collector's usual tactics, asked the price of almost every-thing before she came to the kettle. When she said, " And how much is that? " and the dealer answered " Fifteen cents," she could hardly believe her ears. She hesitated, as if debating, and then said in an off-hand manner, " well, I suppose I might as well take it." Just as she was leaving she said, " You haven't any other, have you? " The dealer brought out another, somewhat smaller, and, watching her face with the shrewdness of his race, saw that she could not conceal her pleasure, and went up five cents in his price! She was preparing to carry off her spoils when he brought out a third, which was in splendid condi-tion, and the smallest of the three. When she asked

"How much?" she found that the market had risen, for he demanded thirty-five cents. It is needless to say that she paid it cheerfully, and I do not think that it would be possible to pick up any more bargains in brass kettles of that junk-man, at least. If you get or have kettles of this kind, do not make the fatal mistake of having feet put upon them, or of having the bail handle taken off and lion's heads put in its place. If you do you will absolutely destroy the whole charm of the thing, and might as well go to any house-furnishing or department store and get a brand-new one. These brass kettles are highly prized to stand on the hearth to hold coal or on the piazza to hold plants. They take a splendid polish, and are brilliant ornaments anywhere.

I have spoken of sugar-bowls of brass. One of these is shown in Figure 71. It is quite pretty, with a pattern on it, and with cast brass handles, which are soldered on. By it stands a brass pitcher, quite a crude affair with an awkward handle, but it is handmade, and as I turn it over I wonder if some "handy man" did not make it for his wife, to eke out their scanty supply of table furniture.

But almost more beloved and sought by the collector than these old articles which we have just shown, and which should be of the first importance with us, are the Russian brasses and coppers which are being brought into the country by every arriving vessel with emigrants, and which are also being made in many a dark cellar on the East Side, New York. It is only a few years since the first of these articles was seen here,

Fig. 72. RUSSIAN SAMOVAR

when a wise Russian who had lived here some years made a return trip to his home and brought back all the old brass objects he could lay his hands on. So successful was his venture that he repeated it many times, and now he is on hand when the ships arrive and buys much of the best that is brought by the immigrants. The every-day Russian kitchen is enough to make the average collector wild with envy, for hanging in rows on its walls are all the kitchen utensils, copper and brass being the common metals in use, the bride bringing enough on her marriage to last all her life. These kitchen utensils are the gift of the bride's mother, who begins to get them together while the daughter is yet a child.

Among the articles most in use in a Russian household is a samovar, and three styles are illustrated in Figures 72-74. In Figure 74, besides the samovar, there are a queer Chinese candlestick and a vessel used at Jewish feasts for sprinkling the guests at table with incense. The vase on the other side is a fine piece of work, and has an inscription of some sort upon it.

In Figure 75 is a Russian brazier, very solid and heavy, with a wrought cover perforated to permit the heat to escape. It is ornate, and on the handles is a mask of a man's face, while on the upper part of the cover is some fine engraving.

It seems hardly proper to leave the subject of brass without at least a reference to one of its most important uses. This was the making of bells. From remote times these were used in religious ceremonials, and their antiquity is unmistakable. In Exodus xxviii, 34, we read a description of the robe of the high priest at the celebration of sacrifices. He was to wear "a golden bell and a pomegranate upon the hem of the robe round about." Apparently it was more than an embroidered ornament, for the next verse says, "His sound shall be heard when he goeth in unto the holy place before the Lord, and when he cometh out."

The early bells used in the Christian Church were hand bells, and some very ancient ones are preserved in Ireland, Scotland, and Wales. They are four-sided, nearly square, and of beaten brass bronzed over. In ancient and more superstitious days the bells of a church were baptised for the purpose of "driving away divils and tempests," as one old writer puts it, though with what success he neglects to state.

The union of copper and tin in different proportions brings about wonderfully different results. In one case it produces bronze; in another speculum-metal, which is brilliantly white and is used for the reflectors of telescopes; while in other proportions it makes bell-metal. Some bells are cast with a proportion of four parts of copper to one of tin. Others have thirty-two per cent. of copper to nine of tin. Lead, zinc, or arsenic are added also. Peter Van der Gheyn was the most famous bell-founder in Flanders in the seventeenth century. He used the choicest metal in his bells,—red copper. Drontheim (called "Rosette," owing to a certain rare pink bloom which seems to lie all over it, like the bloom on a plum or a

Fig. 73. URN

grape) combined with the purest tin. Enthusiasts watching the casting of bells have thrown into the cauldron rings, bracelets, and even bullion. At a certain critical moment zinc and other metals in certain proportions—secrets of each bell-founder—are cast in. Later the bell-pit is flooded, and when the metal is cooled the bell is extracted from the mould. A perfect bell, when struck, yields one note. Even the greatest makers were not exempt from failure, and sometimes, though the bell be perfect, it will crack when being hung, or shortly after.

The bells of Belgium were used for other than religious purposes, since that country was for years a battle-ground. The first necessity in a fortified town was a tower from which the approach of an enemy could be seen; the second, a bell to call the citizens together. In fact the bell in many a church tower did not belong to the cathedral chapter, but to the town. Thus the Curfew, the Carolus, and the St. Mary bells in Antwerp cathedral belong to the town, while the rest belong to the chapter. The Carolus, the best beloved of all the forty bells in Antwerp cathedral, was given by Charles V, and weighs seven and a half tons. It is actually composed of gold, silver, and copper, and is estimated to be worth $100,000. From always striking in the same place, the clapper has worn the two sides greatly, and so careful are the Anversois of their treasure that it is now rung but twice a year.

Two of the most famous English makers of bells were the Penningtons, and Abel Rudall, of Gloucester, whose Christian name was often used in punning fashion on his bells. Latin and rhyming inscriptions were the most popular, and a favourite one was,

> " I to the Church the living call,
> And to the Grave do summon all."

Another favourite inscription in both English and Latin wording was: " Jesu mercy, Lady help."

The bells of St. Paul's, London, are four in number, and the largest bears the inscription: " Richard Phelps made me 1716." In Westminster Abbey are seven bells. On the largest is this inscription: " Remember John Whitmell, Isabel his wife, and William Rus, who first gave this bell, 1430." Then below comes this one: " Newcast in July 1599, and in April 1738, Richard Phelps and T. Lester, Fecit." The oldest bell in this tower dates from 1583. The famous big bell in this same Westminster Tower is cracked, but it is nevertheless dearly loved by the London folk who are used to hear it, even though it does not ring true.

Although England and Belgium seem to be abundantly supplied with bells, it is in Russia that the greatest number and largest-sized ones are to be found, every church having a complete set. Moscow alone is said to possess seventeen hundred.

There are many bells with histories in America, where they served to warn the settlers in the field of the approach of his deadly enemy, the Indian, as well as to call to prayer on Sunday. Few sets of bells have, however, lived through so many vicissitudes as those which now hang in St. Michael's Church, Charleston,

Fig. 74. RUSSIAN SAMOVAR
From the Collection of Mrs. Charles P. Barry

Fig. 75. RUSSIAN BRAZIER

S. C. This in brief is their history. The bells are eight in number, and the first time that they were tolled was for the funeral of Mrs. Martha Grimké, September 22, 1764. For nearly twenty years their work seems to have been more or less peaceful, and when next we hear of them it was as follows:

"At the evacuation of Charles Town, December, 1782, Major Traille, of the Royal Artillery, took down the bells and carried them away as being public property. The next year Sir Guy Carleton ordered them restored immediately."

The bells, however, had been sold in England, and, as it happened, were purchased by a former merchant of Charleston named Ryhiner, as a commercial adventure, and shipped back to that city. On their landing, "the over-joyed citizens took possession of them and hurried them up to the church and into the steeple, without thinking that they might be violating a private right."

"In 1838 two of the bells were found to be cracked; they were sent to England, recast, and returned August, 1839. In June, 1862, they were sent to Columbia, S. C., and stored there. When that city was burned during the occupation by Sherman's army, the bells were burned too. In 1866 the fragments were gathered together and sent to Mears & Steinbank of London, England, the successors of the original founders, and recast in the same moulds. They were sent back to Charleston, and on March 21, 1867, the familiar music of the chimes was heard again, in the strains of 'Home again, home again from a foreign shore.'"

PART IV

COPPER UTENSILS

PART IV

COPPER UTENSILS

THOUGH brass is but a compound of copper and another metal, I treated it first, since, in considering the use of the two materials for domestic utensils, I find brass greatly preponderating over copper in the production of such vessels.

Copper is as widely distributed in nature as iron, but owing to the difficulty of reducing iron from the ore, an acquaintance with that metal comes after the use of copper, silver and gold. Copper occurs in all soils and in many substances as well, such as sea-weed, also in many food-stuffs, etc. The methods of working it vary according to the nature of the ores treated and to local circumstances. It is abundant in America and has been worked from very remote periods.

It is exceedingly malleable and ductile, and exceeds both silver and gold in its tenacity. As we know, it takes a beautiful polish, and I have found that it was used for vessels and ecclesiastical objects almost as much as brass. In an inventory of what were called " Jewels," belonging to the Church of St. Peter, Woking, England, in the year 1587, I find a number of different metals in use, among them copper. Nor was this unusual.

"Imprimis. A pix of silver. VIII oz.
Item. four chalices, parcell gilte thirti oz.
Item. III corporax clothes and their cases.
Item. III alter clothes of velvet and silke.
Item. III aulter clothes of lynnen.
Item. vestimentes.
Item. II coopes of velatt.
Item a surplice and IIII rochettes.
Item. a desk cloth.
Item. II canype clothes, 33 crosse clothes, a crosse staffe.
Item. V towells, a red silke cloth quilted.
Item. a canype of silke.
Item. IIII tumacles and III albes, a crose of copper, a sense⸱
Item. II waterpooles.
Item. V candlestickes.
Item. a latten bason and an ewere. a crosse cloth.
Item. VIII streamars and banners. a font cloth.
Item. II braunches of yron for tapers.
Item. V grete bells in the stepule, IIII little smal bells.
Item. a saunce bell, a payre of orgaynes."

The only article of silver in this enumeration is the pix, and even iron was not deemed too humble a metal for use on the "aulter."

Before touching on the domestic vessels of copper with which we are most likely to be familiar, I wish to show a thurible or *encensoir* (Figure 77) supposed to belong to the fourteenth century, and now in the United States. The common form of censer was either carried in the hand or swung from the hand by chains. This one stands upon a tray, the very beautifully pierced top allowing the incense to escape. It is of a rosy copper colour, heavy and hand made, the design being decidedly Oriental in conception. It looks as if at some time it might have belonged in a mosque, and have looked down on prostrate worshippers with

Fig. 76. KITCHEN AT VAN CORTLAND MANOR

Fig. 77. COPPER THURIBLE
In the Chicago Museum of Fine Arts

flowing robes and turbaned heads. It is very heavy, and the workmanship, notwithstanding its beauty, is extremely crude. It shows the traces of long use, for the incense was sprinkled on hot coals to make it give forth its odour.

The Japanese and Chinese worked in copper centuries ago, and produced many beautiful forms. The Japanese got their copper from China in the shape of ingots, although the metal was well known in Japan from the seventh century.

The Dutch were also workers in copper and exported much of it in ingots as well as in manufactured articles. The uses to which copper was put were not always creditable, for in some instances it was used to debase the coinage. In 1547 the English ordered " 2000 kyntales " of copper from Flanders, to be used in their silver coins. A set of Prussian coins was of copper, silver-coated only, and when, after a time, the silver began to wear off, the accident provoked the remark that " the king's cheeks were blushing for the character of his silbergroschen."

The early adventurers who reached the American continent found that the natives had copper ornaments and implements. Columbus, when at the Cape of Honduras, was visited by a canoe of trading Indians. Among the various articles of merchandise which made up their cargo were " small hatchets, made of copper to hew wood, small bells and plates, crucibles to melt copper, etc."

When the Spaniards first entered the province of Tuspan, Bernal Diaz says:

"Each Indian had beside his ornaments of gold, a copper axe, which was very highly polished, with a handle curiously carved, as if to serve equally for an ornament and for the field of battle. We first thought that these axes were made of an inferior kind of gold; we therefore commenced taking them in exchange, and in two days had collected more than six hundred, with which we were no less rejoiced, not knowing their real value, than the Indians with our glass beads."

La Vega says of the Peruvians:

"They make their arms, knives, carpenter's tools, large pins, hammers for their forges, and their mattocks, of copper which they seek in preference to gold."

Raleigh noted copper ornaments on the Indians of the Carolinas. Granville speaks of copper among the Indians of Virginia. "It was of the colour of our copper, but softer." This was as early as 1585.

Robert Juet, in his account of Hudson's discovery of the river which bears his name, asserts that the savages "had red copper tobacco pipes and other things of copper which they did wear about their necks." He makes mention in another place of "yellow copper," as being distinct from "red copper." In an Indian grave in St. Lawrence County, N. Y., were found spearheads, pointed, double-edged, and a foot long. Two copper-bladed knives were found in the same region.

The Indians of New England, New York, and Virginia had copper implements and ornaments, which were obtained from native deposits, not by smelting the ore. The English pioneers found in the copper

Fig. 78. COPPER WARMING-PAN, KETTLES, ETC.
From the Collection of Mr. Wilford R. Lawshe

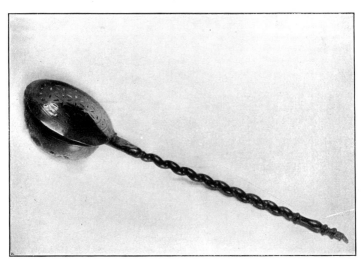

Fig. 79. GEORGE WASHINGTON'S WARMING-PAN
In the National Museum, Washington

Fig. 80. COPPER UTENSILS
In Deerfield Memorial Hall

Fig. 81. PAUL REVERE'S COPPER CHAFING-DISH
In the Rooms of the Antiquarian Society, Concord, Mass.

mines, or pits, masses of copper already at hand, which could be easily worked by the hammer-men who were coming so constantly to America.

Heriot says:

"In two towns 150 miles from the main are found divers small plates of copper, that are made, we are told by the inhabitants, by people who dwell further in the country, where, they say are mountains and rivers which yeild white grains of metal which are deemed to be silver. For confirmation whereof, at the time of our first arrival in the country, I saw two small pieces of silver grossly beaten, about the size of a "tester," hanging in the ears of a Wiroance. The aforesaid copper plates we found to contain silver."

A "tester" was an old coin about the weight of a silver sixpence.

When Massasoit first appeared in Plymouth, in 1621, Edward Winslow, as messenger from the Pilgrims, presented him with some gifts. They were a pair of knives, a chain of copper with a jewel attached; and for Quadequina, the chief's brother, he brought an earring, a pot of strong waters, a good quantity of biscuit, and some butter. The "strong waters," you see, made their appearance early in our bartering with the Indians. Trading went on steadily, and by twenty years later the Indians had acquired some of the vices as well as some of the articles demanded by civilisation.

In 1647 some Nipmuck Indians complained that Uncas's brother, in a raid, had carried away ten of their copper kettles. Copper beads were made by the Indians themselves, and mines are being worked to-day in Mexico which were worked in prehistoric times, as is indicated by the remains of more than two hundred ancient furnaces.

While it is true that copper was found and worked in America, it is also true that it was brought here from other countries in the sheet, or made into utensils. In the ship " John and Sarah," which sailed from London, November 11, 1651, there were shipped to Thomas Kember, of Charlestown, Mass., provisions, iron, metal-work, household utensils, and merchandise. The same merchant, a year previously, had received a cargo of linens and cloths valued at over £2,000.

Not only were utensils made of copper, but buttons were not uncommon. There were snuff and patch boxes, tea-caddies, and other " toys," besides personal ornaments. Kemp, in his " Nine Days' Wonder," describes the host at Rockland with " his black shoes shining and made straight with copper buckles of the best, his garters in the fashion," etc.

Among the articles which I find most often in copper are warming-pans, and they are often very ornamental and have fine handles. We are apt to forget how much suffering must have been caused by the cold houses of a couple of centuries ago, and while it is true that no nation keeps such hot houses as we do, it is also a fact that the houses themselves are warmer.

Among the " Exchequer Papers " in London are many charges for the expenses of " Poor Nelly " Gwynne, who certainly did not come near starving while her royal lover was alive, if these papers are to

Fig. 82.   COPPER KETTLE AND FURNACE
In the Rooms of the Antiquarian Society, Concord, Mass

Fig. 83.   COPPER UTENSILS
From the Collection of Mr. Ralph Burnham

Fig. 84. COPPER POT
From the Collection of Mr. William M. Hoyt

Fig. 85. COPPER KETTLES, RUSSIAN
From the Collection of Mr. Dudley Hoyt

be trusted. Among the bills for the year 1674 there are charges for a French coach and for a great cipher from the chariot-painter; for a bedstead with silver ornaments; for great looking-glasses; for oats and beans; for "chaney" oranges at threepence each; and for cleansing and burnishing the warming-pan! It is somewhat strange that among the few relics of Nelly which are still preserved is a warming-pan, perhaps the very one which was "cleansed and burnished."

Nathaniel Pearsall, of Hempstead, L. I., in 1703 left by special bequest to his five daughters, each a warming-pan, "to be provided by my executors." He does not state whether they were to be of copper or brass, but let us hope that they were of the former metal, since those were so much handsomer. A rather plain example of one of these pans is shown in Figure 78, which has upon it some engraving, and is possibly of Dutch make. In the same picture are some other copper utensils; the long-handled ladle is more often found of brass than of copper, but this one is entirely of copper.

A far handsomer warming-pan is shown in the next illustration, Figure 79, and it has a historical interest as well, for it belonged to George Washington and was in use at Mount Vernon. It is of splendid hue, with a carved mahogany handle, and, besides having seen service, it is worn by frequent cleanings. The pierced work on the cover is fine. Within recent years it has been the fashion to collect such old covers and have them mounted for sconces, with branches for candles arranged on either side. I first saw this use for them in Brussels, but the thrifty Dutch have sent many over here, and you may find them hanging in many a house, the owner of which has not the faintest idea of the homely origin of her "antique" sconces. They have the merit, however, of being really antique. A third pan, with some pretty engraving on it, is shown in Figure 80. The work on these pans is usually of a conventional character, but the engraving on this specimen shows a bird holding what is presumably an olive-branch in its mouth, sitting upon a twig bearing many flowers. The handle is of fine wood, cherry, but is not carved. The copper candlesticks in this picture have a pattern about the base and top, and are not common articles. The pan with the heavy handles was to be used on some sort of a trivet, while the other is merely a bowl. All the articles have seen much service and belong in New England.

Another New England relic is the chafing-dish, or brazier for charcoal, and the kettle which goes with it, to be seen in Figure 81. These were made about the year 1780 by Paul Revere, and in 1875 were given to the Concord Antiquarian Society by his grandson, John Revere. They are of handsome work, as may be seen, the handles of the dish being graceful and massive. We are used to think that the chafing-dish is a product of the modern cooking-school, but it is a very ancient utensil, and there were numerous instances of it in America from the earliest days of the colonies, like the one owned by the widow Cotymore, which is named in her inventory as a "cop. furnace."

Governor Montgomerie's belongings were auctioned

Fig. 86. COPPER UTENSILS, RUSSIAN
From the Collection of Mrs. Charles P. Barry

Fig. 87. COPPER UTENSILS, RUSSIAN
From the Collection of Mrs. Charles P. Barry

Fig. 88. COPPER COFFEE-POTS AND KETTLES, RUSSIAN
From the Collection of Mrs. Charles P. Barry

Fig. 89. COPPER COFFEE-POT AND BOWLS, RUSSIAN
From the Collection of Mrs. Charles P. Barry

off about 1731. Among them were "a large fixt Copper Boyling pot. A large Iron Fire-place, Iron bars and Doors for a Copper." Copper "furnaces" and grates could be bought here by 1751. In 1760 "polished copper chafing-dishes and copper kitchens with stands" were advertised for sale in New York.

Another form of furnace or brazier stands under the copper kettle in Figure 82. This is a more ordinary form of kettle than that made by Paul Revere. The quaint little iron brazier on which it rests is not usual, and was probably made by some workman for his own family. The hot coals were put in the upper perforated part, and the whole contrivance could stand on the floor, the iron shelf preventing the heat from scorching, or hot coals from falling on the boards and setting things on fire, since one of the deadliest enemies of our forefathers was fire, which had to be fought by the most primitive methods. This kettle and stand are also at Concord, but the kettle and measures in the next picture (Figure 83) are at Ipswich, Mass. This style of kettle was quite general, and there were some examples which had an extra part added for standing among the coals. In some instances this lower part was of iron, but in the oldest vessels copper was the metal used throughout the entire kettle, and it was shaped by hand.

I call the two cup-like vessels on the end, "measures," for lack of a better name, and metal measures were in use for dealing out "cyder" as well as "N. E. rum," and every storekeeper was supposed to have a set. The two articles next the kettle have heavier bottoms and show the effects of heat, but they are all fine things, and handsome pieces of metal.

In Figure 91 are shown some quaint old kettles hanging on the crane in the fireplace in Massachusetts Hall, the original building of Bowdoin College. This hall was built in 1802, and in this capacious fireplace, which has remained unchanged since the day the first logs blazed upon its broad hearth, Longfellow did his cooking. The college records do not say whether he was a good cook or not, but he had the best facilities which the college afforded,—an open hearth with swinging crane and glowing coals being considered far superior to the cooking-stoves of that day. He was but fourteen when he entered Bowdoin in the year 1821 and commenced living in this quaint old room.

Another cooking-utensil of primitive make is that in Figure 84, showing most plainly of all the marks of the hammer, and having a cover of similar stout make. It is capable of holding a couple of gallons, and the handles, which are of course rivetted on, are susceptible of lifting a heavy weight. This piece was recently picked up in New York State, and is a most interesting find. Many of these odd pieces were the work of domestic tinkers, or of metal-workers who filled individual orders or made articles which they thought would suit the local market. They are much more interesting to the collector than the conventional shapes, and consequently command higher prices. All the pieces in the next illustration (Figure 85) have a foreign look, except the old teapot at the end. They were spoils from some Polish Jews who were only

Fig. 90. COFFEE-URN
From the Collection of Mrs. David Hoyt.

too glad to exchange them for granite-ware or even tin, and they are now ornamenting a collector's studio.

If you create a demand a supply will spring up to meet it, and the enthusiasm which has developed over Russian coppers and brasses is being catered to. Undoubtedly much fine old ware is being brought into the United States, and if you have the opportunity and desire to seek some pieces from the arriving immigrants, you may obtain them. But to see the artist-artisan at work on his "antiques," visit New York's great Russian quarter, and you will see shop windows shining with thousands of pieces. In Allen Street you will hear the sound of the metal-worker as he swings his mallet, and if you are allowed to penetrate the dusky recesses of the back shop you will find at work a swarthy man with dark eyes, and hanging around him are shears and pincers, hammers and mallets, sheets of copper and patterns by which to cut out his metal. He works at a long rough table, and near at hand is a crude furnace at which he heats his metal, and when it is at the proper temperature to make it malleable, he begins to hammer it into shape, stroke by stroke. As it slowly takes form you see the graceful shapes you admire growing before your eyes, with the hammer-marks which are always so esteemed as showing the work to be hand-made rather than machine-made. To suit "the trade," some of these newly made goods are battered and dented, and hung in the smoke to darken.

A sight by no means uncommon in these shops

in the Ghetto, is that of an old woman of foreign aspect, poking among the articles of brass and copper with which the corners are filled, and muttering to herself in a strange, foreign tongue, as she sets forth one article after another: a great tea-kettle, a cooking-vessel, a pot or two-handled cup,—something that is like the things she was used to at home. She asks the prices, she tries to beat the dealer down, and at last almost sadly replaces the things she has picked out, not able to understand why, as they are old, they should cost so much. Her pennies are few, and the push-cart man just outside has things which will answer her purposes quite as well, and for which she will pay so little.

Figures 86 and 87 show some of these Russian brasses, all of them obtained directly from the peasants themselves. Most of these articles are made from a single piece of copper, but in the worn old kettle in Figure 87 a new bottom has been added, and the upper part has been patched many times. The copper, from much subjection to heat, is almost like parchment and seems ready to crumble at a touch, but it is a beautiful colour, and one wonders at its history. Who knows, perhaps it was carried along in " The Flight of a Tartar tribe." It may have touched Siberia, and come back, but few things even so sturdy as copper kettles have done that!

The tall, graceful, and Oriental-looking coffee-pots shown in Figures 88 and 89 were obtained from the same sources, those in Figure 88 seeming the older. Such pieces as these are great ornaments and seem to

Fig. 91. LONGFELLOW'S FIREPLACE AT BOWDOIN COLLEGE

show best in a dusky corner, whence the gleam of the red copper is very effective.

As the last illustration in this part (Figure 90) I give an American coffee-urn, as widely different in form from the preceding ones as can be imagined. It is about a hundred years old, and was made at the time when "green ivory" was so fashionable for knife-handles, a fancy which did not last long. The knob of the handle of the spout is of this green ivory, and looks very well against the copper hue of the urn itself. One curious detail is that the body is set on at right angles to the base, so that the spout comes at a corner. The coffee is kept hot by putting a hot iron into a receptacle in the inside of the urn, a common way before the use of spirit-lamps. Coffee has had many bad names applied to it, among them being "Polititian's Porridge" and "Mahometan Gruel." Perhaps the latter name could be applied to the fluid which came from the vessels in the former pictures, but I am assured that nothing but the most fragrant beverage ever flowed from this last antique, which even to-day is of use. The hammer-marks are plainly visible on its inner sides, and the pierced work at the top is made by hand and allows the aroma to escape. The collector who owns it worked for months before she could obtain possession of it, and when you come to the matter of price, she becomes very reticent!

PART V

SHEFFIELD PLATE

PART V

SHEFFIELD PLATE

THE city of Sheffield has long been famous for its manufactories, and is known to the world as the place where the best cutlery is made. It was famous for its knives as early as 1380, for at that time Chaucer wrote of the Sheffield "whyttles," as they were then called. In this town, as in so many in England, the changes, both economic and social, from the eighteenth to the beginning of the twentieth century, seem more far-reaching and considerable than those from the sixteenth to the eighteenth century. From the former period (about the year 1700), England progressed by leaps and bounds, and in no one place was this more noticeable than in the smoky city on the Don.

It was not until nearly the close of the first half of the eighteenth century that merchants began to send their wares beyond the narrow confines of their own county, and to seek wider sales for their goods than could be obtained at the annual fairs held in the neighbourhood. Joshua Fox is said to have been the first merchant of Sheffield to enter into personal relations with London, and when in 1723 he started out to make the journey thither, he left behind him a weeping wife and children and uneasy neighbours. He walked the first day as far as Mansfield, and rested there that night and part of the next day, " until travellers met together in sufficient numbers to brave the perils of Nottingham Forest, dreaded both for its robbers and the intricacies of the road."

Even by 1771 London methods were not understood, and Sheffield merchants declined to give a discount, preferring the smaller sales at home. The trade was of course much circumscribed, and consisted chiefly in the preparation of the raw material for the manufacturer. The goods which were made there were sent out to the neighbouring towns by pack-horse, and all the manufactories were small ones.

By 1747 a Mr. Joseph Broadbent took the first step in opening business relations with foreign houses, and his example was followed by other merchants. In 1742 a new trade was added to the large number already practised in the town, which added much to its importance and prosperity, and tended to raise Sheffield to a place among the great industrial centres of England. This trade was the manufacture of plated articles to take the place of silver ones, and though the story of the discovery of silver-plating is an old one, I shall tell it here for the benefit of those who have not heard it before.

"Mr. Thomas Bolsover, an ingenious mechanic, when employed in repairing the handle of a knife, composed partly of copper and partly of silver, was, by the accidental fusion of the two metals, struck with the possibility of uniting them so as to form a cheap substance which should have an exterior of silver, and which might be used for the manufacture of articles which had hitherto been made of silver only. He consequently began a manufacture of articles made of copper, plated with silver, but confined himself to buttons, snuff-boxes, and other light and small articles.

Like many other inventors he did not see the full value of his discovery, and it was reserved for another member of the Corporation of Cutlers of Sheffield, Mr. Joseph Hancock, to show to what other uses copper, plated with silver, might be applied, and how successfully it was possible to imitate the finest and most richly embossed plate. Workmen were secured from among the ingenious mechanics of Sheffield, who in a few years, aided by Mr. Tudor and Mr. Leader and a few other operative silversmiths from London, soon equalled, in the elegance of their designs and the splendour of their ornament, the choicest articles of solid silver."

The manufacture of Old Sheffield Plate has long since died out, and the present metal on which silver is plated is composed of copper, nickel, and zinc, and is white in its tint, while the old ware was plated on copper. The process was interesting, and from an old account of the manufacture, I give the following details.

A number of pounds of copper, say twenty-five or thirty, were put into a melting-pot with some handfuls of charcoal. When the copper was all melted (some manufacturers adding a little brass, the copper alone being too flexible) it was run into a mould of ingot shape, the common size being two and a half inches broad by one and a half inches thick, and in length according to the size of the piece to be made. This ingot was then planed, scraped, and polished perfectly clean and smooth. A sheet of silver, which varied in thickness from one sixteenth to one half of an inch, was then taken, made exactly the same size as the copper ingot to which it was to be applied, and, like the ingot, scraped and cleaned, and made free from any imperfections. The two cleaned surfaces were then put together, great care being taken to avoid handling them.

The next step in the process was to place upon the silver another sheet of copper, about half an inch thick, and somewhat smaller in size than the silver, and then upon the whole was put a strong iron plate, also somewhat smaller than the silver, and not more than half an inch in thickness. These plates were then bound securely together with heavy iron wire, so that they should maintain their relative positions when put into the fire for the process of soldering the silver on the copper. Borax and water was then applied to the edges of the silver, the ingot was placed in a plating-furnace heated with coke, and kept there till the silver was flush around the edge. The ingot was then removed with a pair of specially constructed tongs which did not press into the metal, was placed in a position which kept it perfectly level, and left there till the silver had set. This process was repeated if both sides of the piece to be made required plating, such articles as dish-covers, which were immensely popular at one time, being plated on one side only, the inner side being tinned when the article was made up.

After the ingot was coated with silver, the second step was to roll the ingot to the required thickness, and this was done by passing the ingot through rollers in the usual way. Having got the ingot into sheet metal of the required thickness, the next step was to cut it in a pattern of the article to be made. It is at this stage that the silver shield, which is the best test

Fig. 92. SHEFFIELD-PLATE TRAYS
From the Collection of Mr. H. Coopland, Sheffield, England

Fig. 93. SHEFFIELD-PLATE, CASTORS AND DISHES

of Old Sheffield Plate, was added. If the article to be made was round ware, like cups, teapots, jugs, or urns, the two edges were brought together, being dove-tailed into each other, and then soldered together with filed solid silver. The article then presented the form of a tube, and was put upon what was known as a "stake," and the joining was thoroughly hammered till it was flat and smooth.

The pattern was then given to the workman, and with a tool known as a "bellying-hammer," he brought the body to its greatest diameter, and the other portions to their required shape. It can be seen that this work required a high class of mechanics, and some of these had a habit of going on "sprees," the proprietor advancing the money, often in considerable sums, even a hundred pounds, as the only condition on which the workmen would return, so secure were they of their ability to obtain places. This state of things became intolerable, and as more men learned the work the conditions improved.

All the second step of the work—the bringing the article to its required shape—was called "raising," and the tool was a mallet of horn, while the stake was of steel. After the required shape was obtained, the article was hammered over a number of times, first with a bare hammer, and afterward with a hammer with a steel facing strapped to it, while a pad of cloth was wrapped around the stake, so as to give the article a fine smooth surface.

The feet, handles, or mounts were then added, and this was an elaborate and difficult process, as these pieces were made of a thin sheet of silver struck in a steel die which required great care and expense to get to the proper state of perfection. After being struck, the mounts were filled with solder, and bent, on some soft substance like lead, to the proper shape. They were then soldered on to the article, such as a tray or any round piece like a teapot, a sugar-bowl, etc., the surface around the site of the mount being carefully painted over with whiting, so that the solder should not run on the silvered surface. The object was then carefully heated, and the mounts pressed in place by something soft, like cork, the heat being kept up till the solder was just at the melting-point, but not running, which would ruin the article. After cooling, the whiting was washed off, and the piece was ready for the next step.

This was the addition of the silver edges, which were applied to the body of the article on one side, and passed under the mounts on the other edge, being soldered down on both sides. The article was now ready for the decorator, if it was to be chased, and finally passed into the hands of the burnisher and polisher. The burnishing was done by women with a bit of fine polished steel, worked by hand in different ways. It can be seen that this process of manufacture was elaborate and necessarily expensive.

For the first sixty years after Bolsover's discovery copper was plated on one side only, and when any article had to be plated both inside and out it was made of two sheets of plate, the edges being drawn over so as to expose the silvered sides to view. After a time it was found possible to coat the copper on both sides, and so well do some of these old pieces wear that they are still in splendid condition, showing at the edges only any signs of the copper.

In England the term most frequently applied to this plated ware is " Close Plate," and when the copper shows through at the edges it is known to the trade as " bleeding,"—a very comprehensive term. Although we in America are apt to associate this kind of ware with the city of Sheffield only, the fact remains that it was also made in Birmingham. In that city they seemed to confine themselves largely to the smaller class of articles, like snuff-boxes, buttons, and boxes. In fact Sheffield says that Birmingham has been remarkable for three things only, buttons, buckles, and riots! Certainly when we come to read the history of the city it seems to have made its share of the former, and undoubtedly it had more than its share of the latter.

I have mentioned what an important article of trade buttons were, and though they held the field longer they did not at any time arrive at the importance which buckles held. For at least one hundred and fifty years, buckles played an important part in the dress of every man, woman, and child in Great Britain, and thousands of pairs were exported annually. They first made their appearance about 1659, and were about the size of a bean, for at that time the metals employed were either gold or silver, and while the nobility sported diamonds in their buckles, the middle class were content with paste. In few fashion-books can be found any reference to buckles, yet they flourished till about 1800, rising and falling from the hat to the foot, and they were sometimes to be found on foot, knee, and cap, in the same costume. If you consult the pictures of the old masters, you will find that buckles are lacking in those painted by Van Dyck, are occasionally present in those of Lely and Van Loo, and are ever present in the lovely portraits of Gainsborough, while Sir Joshua Reynolds painted his admirals in small-clothes with long stockings and buckled shoes, a costume which has now disappeared from the navy except on the stage. In Hogarth's striking pictures of life in his time in London, you will find buckles alike on his drunken soldiers, on his apprentices, on the women of that class, and on the "lady-friends" of the soldiers. But among women of the higher classes, such as are pictured in "Marriage à la Mode," they are absent, though in the songs of the period they are often satirized, and one of the dances was called "Cover the Buckle." Pepys, the indefatigable, mentions in his diary for January 22, 1659, "This day I began to put buckles on my shoes."

In the "Toilet of England," it mentions for 1670:

"The Spanish leather boot introduced under Charles I still continues to be the fashion, but the immense Roses on the shoes have gradually declined, and are replaced by wide strings and buckles."

In order to supply those persons who wished, as far as they could, to follow the mode set by the court, the buckle-makers of Sheffield, Birmingham, Wol-

Fig. 94. URNS, WINE-COOLERS, AND TRAYS

verhampton, and many other towns made immense numbers. When the fashion was at its height 2,500,-000 buckles were made at Birmingham alone, and when there was a change in the fashion it caused the greatest apprehension. In the " Annual Register " for December 14, 1791, appears the following note:

" Several respectable buckle-makers from Birmingham, Walsall, and Wolverhampton waited upon H. R. H. the Prince of Wales with a petition setting forth the distressed situation of thousands in the different branches of the buckle trade, from the fashion now and for some time back so prevalent of wearing shoe-strings instead of buckles. H. R. H., after considering the petition very attentively, graciously promised his utmost assistance by his example and influence."

The " Gazette " announces after this appeal:

" The unmanly shoe-string will henceforth be thrown aside for the buckle. On his birthday, his Royal Highness, and all his sisters, appeared in the Soho new-invented shoe latchets, and have since continued to wear them. Indeed no well-dressed gentleman or lady now appears without these buttons, and the ornament of the buckle."

But for all this the shoe-buckle died, and the effeminate shoe-string came in. At the time of their greatest popularity buckles were made from gold, silver-gilt, silver, Sheffield plate, paste (both French and English), brass, copper, glass, jet, pinchbeck, gun-metal, steel, and sometimes wood. Sir S. Ponsonby Fane, long a collector of brass and iron work, has made a collection of these buckles, and has about four hundred. Many of them are of this Old Close Plate and are very ornamental, the plate in some cases being decorated with knobs or buttons of cut steel.

I have, myself, a pair of these old plate buckles which I got years ago in Holland, and which have the two stars of the Soho Plate Works of Birmingham. They have hand-wrought steel points to hold the leather, and beautiful tiny raised stars are the ornament. Every half inch all around the top, there are, besides, cut steel facets, which gleam brightly when they are polished. These buckles "bleed" in many places, and plainly show the silver edges. They are not very large, measuring only two inches across the long way, and they are oval in shape.

In the early days of the Colonies buckles were much worn in America, and many of them were of good gold plate, for it was only the few who could squander much coin on such frivolities as these. What has become of all these millions of shoe-buckles it would be hard to say. As they were small, they were probably thrown into the scrap-heap as entirely worthless, unless they were of paste or some of the more precious metals.

In many of the illustrations of this subject you will see that the article is marked with either initials or a crest. Heraldry has long been a hobby with our English cousins, and we are now taking up the cry, having crests and quarterings made to suit our fancy if we have no such belongings rightfully in the family.

To meet this demand for marking one's possessions which was felt by nearly every would-be purchaser, the Sheffield manufacturer imbedded in his Close Plate a shield of pure silver, so that engraving would not

Fig. 95. TRAYS AND WINE-COOLER

Fig. 96. TABLE ARTICLES AND CANDLESTICKS

there was no chemical affinity between the gold and the object to be coated, it was necessary to use a solution of nitrate of mercury, which was made by using a quart of nitric acid to a tablespoonful of mercury. The union of these substances is accompanied by the production of considerable heat and the formation of nitrous gas. When this nitrate of mercury was put on the copper, its surface at once became an amalgam, and to this surface the other amalgam of gold and mercury closely adhered by means of the molecular attraction of fluid metals to each other. The mode of applying the gold to the interior surfaces of vessels was by coating them with the nitrate and then applying the amalgam. When this was done, the vessels, with the gold side up, were placed in open pans and set over a coke fire, the heat causing the mercury slowly to evaporate and leave the gold only. This process, though a costly one, was lasting, as may be proved by many a piece of plate still bearing its golden interior. The modern way of depositing the gold by electricity, while much cheaper, is far less lasting.

The last and perhaps the most important improvement in the making of Sheffield plate was the process of soldering on solid silver edges and mounts, which protected the parts most exposed to wear and prevented the "bleeding" of the edges. This method was invented by Mr. George Cadman, when in partnership with Mr. Samuel Roberts, about the year 1784.

At least ten years before this, in 1773, the popularity of the Sheffield plate had led to the opening of an assay office in Sheffield, and the production of sterling ware. This was protected by a system of marks which changed with every year.

The marks on Sheffield plate were usually the names of the makers, or their initials, accompanied by some device. Frequently the device appeared alone, and I give some of the best-known ones, hoping that you will find some of them on those old wine-coasters which belonged to your grandfather, or on the tray which held the snuffers for those tall candlesticks which have stood so long on the parlour mantel!

And now to give some idea of the prices at which this old ware changes hands. A pair of wine-coolers, like the one on the left in Figure 93, sold recently in London for £15. Very plain candlesticks for bedroom use bring $7 or $8 a pair, while ornamental ones are worth $25 any day. Such candelabra as that seen in Figure 95—a Sheraton pattern—are cheap at $50 a pair, even though it does hold but two candles, while those in Figures 96 and 98 are worth much more, and are difficult to find in America in the old plate, although the same patterns are reproduced in modern plate.

Old Sheffield ware should never be replated, and articles which have been are worthless to the collector, since the old process, which made the article of worth, has been covered up. In this branch of the antique business, as in all others, the counterfeiter has been at work. The truth is that this is a collecting age, and the curio-dealer is doing all in his power to make it pass quickly by flooding the market with spurious imitations.

These goods are not like the toys and other trifles which are imported, and stamped "Made in Germany," but not only are they not stamped at all, but they are excellent imitations. In this very fact lies the danger to the public, for we may buy both in England and this country "old English glass," made in Holland and Germany, "Battersea" enamels fresh from Paris, "Bow" and "Chelsea" figures which the potteries in Germany are turning out by the hundred, not to mention all the "antique furniture" made here, there, and everywhere, the samplers copied from old ones, and even "Sheffield plate." In this latter case the design is made in copper from a good old pattern, and then "dipped," a few places are rubbed till the copper shows through; some scratches are added by means of a sharp tool; and there is the article, ready for a confiding public. In fact the manufacturers in Sheffield are constantly importuned to "copy" old plate for the benefit of unscrupulous dealers who would not hesitate to palm it off as the "real thing."

The making of Sheffield plate covered about a century, from 1742 to 1845, when the process of electro-plating entirely crowded out the older method. The number and variety of articles manufactured was very great, and comprised *épergnes,* urns for both tea and coffee, teapots, coffee-pots, tea-kettles, lamps, candlesticks and candelabra, tankards and measures of all sizes, mugs, jugs, cups, tumblers, caudle-cups, toast-racks, cruet-frames, hot-water plates, platters and dishes, venison-dishes, dish-rims, covers, castors, crosses, trays and waiters of all sizes, bottle- and writing-stands, tureens, ladles, spoons, scallop-shells for serving fish, canisters, tea-caddies, mustard-pots, argyles, snuffers and trays, wine-funnels, saltcellars of many shapes, bottle-labels, cream-pails, bread-, cake-, and sugar-baskets, skewers, spoon-trays, cream-jugs, lemon-strainers, cheese-toasters, stewpans, saucepans, chocolate-pots, snuff-boxes, bridle-bits, stirrups, spurs, buttons, buckles, knife- and fork-handles, bridle-buttons, saddle-buttons, and a number of other articles.

In Figure 97 is shown a choice collection of tea-pots, all but two showing the fine silver feet, beadings, and mounts which were so prevalent in this high-class work. Some of the pieces are lavishly engraved, and many are fluted, a favourite form of design for many years. It is a pity that there is no way of telling the age of the pieces, for the makers contented themselves with putting on their names or trademarks, and left to the sterling-makers the practice of putting on the date letter.

It is possible to get good old plate in America. Indeed, I know of some pieces which pass for silver. One urn in particular is in my mind which the owners calmly assert is silver, even though in spots the copper is smiling through at you! I long ago gave up setting people right as to their belongings, and can now regard with interest a piece of what I know to be Stafford-shire ware when its owner assures me it is "old Capo di Monti." It is only by special request that it is safe to " name and date antiques," and you want to be very sure of your collector even then. In Figure 102 are

Fig. 97.   TEA AND COFFEE POTS

Fig. 98.   CANDLESTICKS AND COVERS

some nice old plated teapots, which, though unmarked, I believe to be Sheffield, since they have all the proper characteristics, silver mounts, silver beadings, and are plated on copper. They are not so old as the specimens given in Figure 97, for this squatty pattern was popular after 1800. The central teapot is not to be considered, as it is silver; but all three pieces belong to one collector, and he had that one put in too.

Several times within late years it has been possible to get fine old Sheffield plate at Washington, where English ambassadors or members of their embassy have sold off many of their household goods before returning to England. I know of two dishes that were obtained in this way. They have on them a well-known crest, and are handsome and fine pieces, similar in pattern to the little one on the right in the upper row of Figure 99. The handles of most of these dishes unscrew, and the cover can be used as a dish also.

Figure 99 contains many interesting pieces, the splendid caudle-cups on the lower row, and the quaint old egg-stand, a pattern once seen on every well-appointed breakfast-table, standing cheek-by-jowl with the toast-rack. The two little saltcellars standing on the same row with the toast-rack were favourites too, and contained red or blue glass cups to hold the salt. The tall perforated basket near one of the salts was for sugar, and also had a glass receptacle in it. There are two mustard-pots in the row below, the one with the flat cover being a pattern which was copied in both pewter and Britannia ware.

I regard as the handsomest pieces of all, those shown in Figure 100. Note the exquisite chasing on the two waiters, as well as the heavy moulded borders, which are of silver. The two cake-baskets speak for themselves, and the cover, though not very large, is vastly more elegant than was common. Two other cake-baskets—very choice specimens, too—may be seen in Figure 94, this style of dish seeming to be one on which much ornament was lavished. It is a pity such pretty articles of table furniture are no longer "the thing."

In its best days Sheffield plate was by no means considered "second cut," so to speak, for articles made in it were presented to dignitaries on great and special occasions. Lord Nelson had an inkstand of Sheffield plate, which consisted of an oval stand with a perforated rim which stood up all around, and inside were two round, plain bottles, one for ink and one for sand. In the centre was a cup for wafers, and forming a cover to it was a bell. The admiral used this inkstand on board the "Elephant," at the battle of Copenhagen in 1801. There is a little story connected with this inkstand which the owner of it tells with unction. Just before the battle a Danish officer came aboard the flagship, to see if the British admiral had any proposals to make to the king of Denmark. Having occasion to express his errand in writing, he found the quills blunt, and, holding one up, is reported to have said, "If your guns are no better pointed than your pens, you will make little impression on Copenhagen." Later in the day, when the victory was

Fig. 99.   TABLE UTENSILS AND CANDLE-CUPS

Fig. 100.   CAKE-BASKETS AND TRAYS

practically accomplished, Lord Nelson himself had occasion to use the inkstand to dictate terms to his opponents, and the story does not say that he found any difficulty with the pens. The result of this victory was the capture of six line-of-battle ships, eight prams, all of which were either burned or sunk, except the " Holstein," which was sent home under the charge of Captain James Clarke, to whom Lord Nelson gave the inkstand as a memento of the occasion. On it is engraved, " Admiral Lord Nelson to Captain James Clarke, H. E. I. C. S." On the handle of the bell is " Copenhagen, 1801." On the other side is the monogram of the admiral, H.N. surmounted by a coronet. It is pleasant to know that this trophy has never passed out of the hands of the family of Captain Clarke, and that it is now treasured by one of his descendants. It was not possible to obtain a photograph of this inkstand, which is in England, and I think it must have been made on a special order, for I have never seen any other like it or resembling it.

The collection on which I have drawn most heavily for illustrating Sheffield plate is that which belongs to Mr. Henry Coopland, Glossop Road, Sheffield, England. He has had unusual opportunities for collecting specimens, and he began to gather them before they had become as popular as they are now. Only a small part of his immense collection is shown, and it is known throughout England as the finest one outside of London. The Viscountess Wolseley is another great collector, and many of her specimens are marked, as are Mr. Coopland's, with the best-known names of makers of this ware. W. & G. Siddons, whose firm goes back to 1784, is represented in both collections, and so are Fenton, Creswick, & Co., and Holy, and Hoyland. I have often been asked how it is possible to know Sheffield plate. The copper body is always one of the sure tests, as well as the silver edges and mounts, and the presence of the silver shield, which often stands out boldly when the rest of the silver is much worn off. You can see it plainly in the tray on the left hand in Figure 92, and even when the silver plating is quite intact you can detect the presence of the shield by breathing upon the place where the crest or initials are engraved. The moisture will stand longer on the shield than on the surrounding surface.

The urn in Figure 103 is not a common pattern, yet it is Sheffield ware, and what our grandmothers would have called "the best plate." The shield is quite evident with the lettering and a wreath of ornament surrounding it; the beading and lions' heads are of silver; and the only places where it "bleeds" is on the base. The coffee was kept hot by the iron piece inside, and the urn is far handsomer than it looks in the picture. This urn is owned in New York State, but I know of another in California, exactly like it, with the same ornament around the shield, but of course with different initials, which was brought home from England by a sea-captain to his wife, as a present after a prosperous voyage. This was early in 1800, and it is now owned by the grandson of the original purchaser.

None of the really old urns had lamps to keep the

Fig. 101.   CANDLESTICKS

Fig. 102.   TEAPOTS

coffee warm, and those which have were among the latest pieces of this plate made.

The subject of candlesticks is one of much interest, for there are so many patterns to be had, some of them of much beauty, like the one in the centre of Figure 94, which was also an *épergne,* down to the bedroom lights, one of which may be seen in Figure 101. The one to which I refer in this picture is the small one standing on the box. It is of Sheffield plate and was bought within a few months at a sale of an old English manor-house. The tall shade is an ample provision against drafts, and the extinguisher has a handle so long that it can be dropped down even if the candle has burned down quite into the socket. Even though it has no place here, I should like to mention that the other stick is one of a pair got at the same time and place as the little one, and is of solid mahogany, the shade being of old English ground glass. Nobody knew how long they had been fixtures in that old house, but the wood is quite black and has a superb polish. These candlesticks stand thirty inches high.

The last illustration which I show is what is known as a venison-dish. The cover rolls back under the bottom when not in use, and there is a receptacle for hot water in the bottom. There is a perforated tray on which the venison is placed, and the whole thing is a choice piece of work. An ivory button in the handle stands out so that the cover could be turned over without burning the fingers. There is a shield which has never been used.

This piece was secured in America by a collector

who has the gift of finding much that is rare and beautiful. She can no longer get her things for that " song " which was once so proverbial, but pays quite high prices, since owners have a better idea of the value of what they wish to sell. Besides having much old furniture, pewter, plate, and glass, she has a collection of eighteen mirrors, those delightful old things with pictures painted in the upper panels. Some of these mirrors are in mahogany frames, some in gilt, some combine the two, but all of them are handsome, one or two are elegant, and all are desirable. When you point out to her that she has far too many for her own good, she always answers that when she has twenty-four she is going to stop, and that then perhaps she will part with some. She has collected so much that she has got the speech, no one ever " sells " an antique; they always " part " with it.

Among the small things in good old plate which are not uncommon in America are snuff-boxes and patchboxes. I come across them frequently, and they are almost always examples of choice work. There were some manufacturers in Sheffield who made nothing but these small articles, and as it was so much the mode to take snuff, every one with any pretensions to style had to have one. Among the advertisements in our old papers I do not find any allusions to Sheffield plate. The term " plate " is sometimes used, but in England this refers to silver, not to plated ware, and I have taken it for granted that the advertisers meant the solid ware, as they were in most cases merchants from London. There is one article which we know

Fig. 103.   COFFEE-URN

Fig. 104.   VENISON DISH

was much esteemed during the times of the Georges, when this old plate was in its prime, which I do not find mentioned in any list of articles made at Sheffield, nor have I ever seen an old one, though modern examples are plenty. That is a punch-bowl. That there were plenty of them is true, but they seem to have been made of silver or china, and there are a number of very rich silver ones to be found among the old families in America.

Another article—small, this time,—is to be found very rarely. It is also connected with the flowing bowl, and by its means it was possible for the traveller at any time to have a cup of negus, or any other of those spiced drinks with which our ancestors were wont to solace themselves. This small article was a nutmeg-holder, or spice-box. It was trifling in size, with a lid the interior of which was rough enough for the nutmeg to be grated upon it. No drink from "Bishop's Sleeves" to "Oxford night-caps" but had its final touch added by the spice-box, and these pretty trifles of Sheffield or sterling silver were popular enough with the fashionable blade, who regarded himself as quite *à la mode* when he had his spice-box in one pocket and his snuff-box in the other.

The spice-box, the snuff-box, and the patch-box have long since lost their usefulness, but we treasure them the more for the pictures they bring to the mind's eye of those brave old days under the Georges.

SHEFFIELD MANUFACTURERS OF CLOSE PLATE

FROM THE LATTER PART OF THE EIGHTEENTH CENTURY TO 1845

ASHWORTH, ELLIS & CO.
BANBURY, THOMAS, *Norfolk St.*
ELLIOTT, THOMAS, *Jehu Lane*
ELLIS, THOMAS, *Norfolk St.*
FENTON, CRESWICK & CO., *Mulberry St.*
GREAVES, JOHNABAB, *Snuff-box Maker*
HANCOCK, ROWBOTTOM & CO.
HOLY, DANIEL, WILKINSON & CO., *Mulberry St.*
HOYLAND, JOHN & CO., *Mulberry St.*
KIRK, JOSEPH, *Mulberry St.*
LAW, THOMAS & CO., *Norfolk St.*
MARGRAVE, MARSDEN & CO.
MARSDEN, WILLIAM
MARTON, THOMAS
ROBERTS, EYRE, BELDON & CO., *Union St.*
ROWBOTTOM, I. & CO.
TONKS, WILLIAM
TUDOR & LEADER, *Sycamore Hill*
WILSON, JAMES
WINTER, PEARSON & HALL.

W. & G. Sissons. 1784

Walker, Knowles & Co.

Fenton, Creswick & Co.

Watson
(now W. Padley & Sons)

Henry Wilkinson & Co.

Soho Plate, Birmingham.

Daniel Holly & Co.

Boulton, Birmingham.

APPENDIX

APPENDIX

The following lists have been compiled from Masse's "Pewter Plate"; Welch's "List of Freemen"; Touch-Plates in Pewterers' Hall; Wood's "Scottish Pewter"; and from many specimens of ware.

MARKS AND NAMES FOUND ON FOREIGN PEWTER

Brussels
Gothic B, crowned, in a shield
St. Michael and the Dragon in a beaded circle
Six-petalled rose, crowned
G. Pierre, Bruxelles, in oval with two stars
J. B. Y., with crowned rose (Eighteenth century)

Lille
Albert et Mulie à Lille

Liège
Angel in oval
Rose with L. L.

Antwerp
Arms with hand
Rose alone or crowned
Joseph Berton, 1777
M. A. Hagen's Blok Zinn

Germany
Melchior Koch

Nuremberg
Jorg Christian, 1550
Nicholas Horcheimer, 1570
Melchior Horcheimer, 1583
Paulus Böhem, 1585
Sebaldus Reuter, 1611
Michael Rössner, 1620
Lorenz Appel, 1630

France
Paris marks:
An angel with "Paris" in crown
Crowned rose
Fleur-de-lys
French makers of pewter:
Jehan de Montrousti, 1400
Jehan Lampène, 1484
Hector Drouet, 1487
Jehan Anot, 1555
Christofle Fromont, 1668, Pewterer to the King
Guillaume Couetteau, 1677
Geoffroy et Helot, 1745
Renaud et Cie, 1760
Boileau fils, 1772
Parain, 1789

LIST OF ENGLISH PEWTERERS
FROM 1500 TO 1600

Abraham, Henry, 1571
Afferton, John, 1506
Alexander, Paul, 1516
Anayson, John, 1523
Ashlyn, Lawrence, 1559
Astlyn, John, 1514
Astlyn, Lawrence, 1504
Astlyn, Walter, 1534

Baker, William, 1558
Barker, John, 1585
Baxter, John, 1513
Bennett, Ph., 1542
Beswick, Thomas, 1533
Blackwell, Thomas, 1547
Boultinge, John, 1575
Burton, John, 1513

Cacher, Edward, 1556
Callie, William, 1510
Carnadyne, Alex., 1595
Carrye, John, 1543
Catcher, John, 1585
Chamberlayn, Thos., 1517
Chawner, Robt., 1573
Chyld, John, 1534
Clark, Henry, 1555
Clark, Thos., 1543
Crostwayt, Rich., 1541
Crostwayte, Nich., 1557
Crowe, Wm., 1512
Crowson, John, 1586
Curtis, Thos., 1538
Curtis, Wm., 1573
Curtys, Peter, 1525
Curtys, William, 1566

Draper, James, 1598
Droke, William, 1528
Dropwell, Robt., 1570

Eastwell, Abraham, 1591
Elyot, Thos., 1579
Emmeston, Wm., 1591

Fenn, George, 1588
Ferner, John, 1595
Flood, John, 1537
Foster, Boniface, 1574
Foull, Thos., 1541

Gardner, Allyn, 1578
Gartwell, Abraham, 1595
Gasker, Percival, 1593
Goodman, Philip, 1596
Greenfell, George, 1579

Haroye, John, 1555
Harper, Edward, 1572
Hawcliff, Symon, 1568
Hawke, Thomas, 1588
Hawkins, Stephen, 1543
Haynes, William, 1560
Heythwaite, Mighell, 1553
Hustwaite, Robt., 1571
Hustwayte, Wm., 1548
Hyll, Wm., 1599
Hylyngworth, Clement, 1553

Isade, Roger, 1569

Jackson, John, 1589
Jann, Thos., 1535

Jardeine, Nicholas, 1573
Jaxon, William, 1512

King, Richard, 1593

Langtoft, Nicholas, 1524
Langtoft, Robt., 1519
Loton, William, 1567

Machyn, Thos., 1539
Makyns, Walter, 1554
Mannynge, Rich., 1574
Mansworth, Thos., 1585
Mathewe, John, 1569
Mears, William, 1598
Mills, Nicholas, 1534
Mylls, William, 1564

Newes, Robt., 1578
Nicholls, Thos., 1566
Nixon, Robt., 1589
Nogay, Thos., 1580
Norton, John, 1583

Onton, John, 1513
Outlawe, Thos., 1504

Pecke, Nicholas, 1548
Pecok, Thos., 1511
Pecok, William, 1510
Perkyns, Rich., 1593
Ponder, Simon, 1555

Redman, William, 1574

Renston, John, 1527
Reo, Edward, 1582
Rowe, William, 1507
Rowlandson, Stephen, 1563
Roysdon, John, 1526
Royston, John, 1558

Scott, Rich., 1562
Sherwyn, John (1), 1547
Sherwyn, John (2), 1578
Steward, John, 1595
Stode, Joseph, 1530
Straye, Ralph, 1587

Taylor, Richard, 1524
Taylor, Robt., 1551
Thompson, R., 1576
Thurgood, John, 1503

Urswyke, Thos., 1533

Waddoce, Thos., 1565
Wargnyer, Rich., 1561
Waryng, John, 1555
Whytbe, Thos., 1551
Williamson, Rich., 1553
Willis, Nich., 1529
Wilson, John, 1502
Wood, Robert, 1551
Wood, Thos., 1592
Wood, William, 1589
Wynsley, John, 1525

FROM 1600 TO 1700

W. A., 1663
W. A., 1682
Abbott, John, 1693
Adams, Henry, 1692
Adams., Nath., 1692
Adams, Robt., 1667

Adams, William, 1671
Alder, Thos., 1667
Allen, John, 1671
Allen, Richard, 1668
Angell, Philemon, 1691
Archer, William, 1653

Atlee, W., 16—
Austin, Samuel, 1693
Austin, William, 1677
Aylife, William, 1667

D. B., 1670
I. B., 1665
I. B., 1699
Baker, Samuel, 1678
Balleson, Thos., 1667
Barrow, Richard, 1667
Barton, Dan., 1678
Baskerville, John, 1695
Bateman, John, 1670
Beard, Sampson, 1691
Bearsley, Job, 1678
Bennett, John (1), 1653
Bennett, John (2), 1679
Bennett, William, 1662
Benton, Ralph, 1681
Blackwell, Daniel, 16—
Blagrave, Wm., 1664
Blunt, John, 1681
Bonkin, Jonathan, 16—
Bowyer, William, 1642
Boyden, Benj., 16—
Bradstead, H., 16—
Brailsford, Peter, 1667
Brettell, James, 16—
Brill, Henry, 16—
Brocklesby, Peter (1), 1629
Brocklesby, Peter (2), 1637
Brocklesby, Peter (3), 1667
Brooks, John, 1637
Brooks, Rich., 1667
Browne, Martin, 16—
Byran, Edgerton, 16—
Bull, John, 1678
Bullevant, Jas., 1667
Burt, Luke, 16—

Burt, Thos., 1630
Burton, William, 1685
Butcher, Gabriel, 1633
Butcher, Robt., 1639
Butcher, Thos., 1652
Buxton, Robt., 1619
Byrd, John, 1654

B. C., 1651
C. C., 1672
G. C., 1676
T. C., 1663
W. C., 1663
Cambridge, Job, 1687
Campion, John, 1662
Carter, Thos., 1648
Castle, John, 16—
Chassey, Jos., 1650
Chesslin, Rich., 1682
Chester, Geo., 1628
Childe, John, 1643
Claridge, Benj., 1672
Clark, John, 1667
Cliffe, Thomas, 1639
Clyffe, John, 1602
Cock, Humphrey, 1670
Cole, Benj., 1683
Cole, Jeremiah, 1692
Collier, Nich., 1604
Collyer, Rich., 1669
Cooper, Benj., 1684
Coursey, John, 1667
Cowdwell, John, 1620
Cowes, Henry, 1640
Cowes, Thomas, 1605
Cowley, William, 1695
Cowyer, Nicholas, 1607
Cox, John, 1679
Cox, Richard, 1656
Cranley, Charles, 16—

Crookes, William, 16—
Cropp, William, 1667
Cross, William (1), 1659
Cross, William (2), 1668

E. D., 1672
F. D., 1672
I. D., 1668
R. D., 1677
W. D., 1668
Davis, Rich., 1664
Dawes, Rich., 1652
Dawkins, Pollisargus, 1628
Dickenson, Thos., 1669
Dimocke, William, 16—
Diston, Giles, 1667
Ditch, William, 1669
Drinkwater, Timothy, 1676
Drury, John, 1673
Duffield, Peter (1), 1672
Duffield, Peter (2), 1697
Dunne, Rich., 1696
Dunninge, Thos. (1), 1604
Dunning, Thos. (2), 1617
Durand, Jonas, 1699
Duxell, Rich., 1616
Dyer, Lawrence, 1675
Dyer, William, 1667

B. E., 1664
G. E., 1663
I. E., 1686
Eames, Rich., 1697
Elliot, Thos., 1604

A. F., 1646
H. F., 1668
Fly, William, 1691
Fox, Edward, 1617
Freeman, Henry, 1669

French, John, 1687
Fullham, Andrew, 1614
Fullham, John, 1637

Gavokeford, 1601
Gilbert, Edw., 1662
Gisborne, Robert, 1691
Glover, Edw., 1620
Glover, Henry, 1620
Glover, Richard, 1606
Glover, Roger, 1615
Godfrey, Stephen, 1679
Graham, Basill, 16—
Grainger, William, 1638
Graunt, Joseph, 1659
Graves, Francis, 1629
Green, William, 1684
Gregg, Robt., 1683
Gregg, Thos., 1671
Groome, Randell, 1624
Gruwin, Gabriel, 1693

I. H., 1663
R. H., 1664
T. H., 1676
Hadley, Isaac, 1668
Hale, Geo., 1675
Hamilton, Alexander, 1646
Hand, Samuel, 16—
Harding, Robert, 1668
Harendon, ——, 1664
Harford, Henry, 1696
Hartshorne, Michael, 1693
Hatch, Henry, 16—
Hatfield, Wm., 1627
Haveland, Miles, 1664
Haward, Thos. (1), 1666
Haward, Thos. (2), 1667
Hawkes, Edw., 1667
Heath, Edw., 1656

Heath, John, 1618
Heath, Richard, 1699
Henson, Thomas, 1614
Hickling, Thomas, 1698
Hicks, Thomas, 1698
Hill, Hough, 1625
Hill, William, 1672
Hills, William, 1636
Hodges, Jos., 1667
Hodgkis, Arthur, 1635
Hollford, Stephen, 1668
Holt, John, 16—
Hopkins, Jos., 1667
Howell, Ralph, 1623
Huil, Thos., 1650
Hulls, Ralph, 1682
Hunton, Nich., 1670
Hurdman, Wm., 1622
Hyatt, Humphrey, 1681
Hyll, Walter, 1601

E. I., 1675
H. I., 1675
I. I., 1666
R. I., 1696
Iles, Rich., 1697
Ingles, John, 1678
Ingole, Dan., 1688

Jackson, Sam'l, 1684
Jackson, Thos., 1660
Jackson, William, 1668
Jacobs, John, 1663
Jacomb, Josiah, 1675
Jarrett, John, 1656
Johnson, John, 1666
Jones, James, 1628
Jones, Owen, 1647
Jones, Robt., 1667
Jones, Thos., 1632

Jones, William, 1676

T. K., 1672
Kelk, James, 1687
Kelke, Nicholas, 1665
Kent, William, 1623
King, Abraham, 1693
King, Thomas, 1687
Knight, Francis, 1692
Knowles, Tobias, 1664

I. L., 1663
I. L., 1684
Lackford, John, 1664
Langford, William, 1679
Langley, Adam, 1680
Larkin, Francis, 1685
Lawrence, Stephen, 1684
Lea, Francis, 1664
Leach, Thomas, 1691
Leapidge, Edward, 1699
Leapidge, Thomas, 1696
Leeson, John, 1680
Leeson, Robert, 1648
Lock, Robert, 1692
Long, Sefton, 1680
Long (2), Sefton, 1692
Lucas, Robert, 1667

A. M., 1679
I. M., 1662
N. M., 1640
W. M., 1666
Mabbes, Sam'l, 1685
Major, John, 1657
Mann, John, 1688
Marsh, Ralph, 1662
Marsh (2), Ralph, 1679
Marshall, Thomas, 16—

Marten, Robert, 1674
Mason, John, 1695
Mason, Richard, 1679
Mathews, Peter, 1632
Mathews, William, 1689
Mathews, William, 1699
Maundrill, Richard, 1693
Mayor, Anthony, 1668
Meares, John, 1657
Meares, Ralfe, 1643
Meggot, George, 1655
Mellett, Rich., 1660
Mills, Nathan, 1668
Milton, Wheeler, 1650
Mitchell, John, 1619
Modson, Richard, 1667
Molton, John, 1665
Momford, John, 1641
Moulins, Robt., 1676
Mullins, R., 1647
Munns, Nathaniel, 1667

I. N., 1678
Needham, Thos., 1665
Newman, Michael, 1652
Newman, Michael, Jr., 1670
Newman, Thos., 1660
Newnam, Thos., 1642
Newton, Hugh, 1616

F. P., 1680
I. P., 1693
P. P., 1668
W. P., 1663
W. P., 1698
Page, John, 1697
Paine, ———, 1661
Palmer, Roger, 1642
Paltock, John, 1627
Parke, Peter, 1666

Parker, Joseph, 1679
Parrett, Thomas, 1609
Pauling, Henry, 1659
Paxton, William, 1696
Perris, Henry, 1678
Peltiver, William, 1679
Philips, James, 1651
Piddle, Joseph, 1685
Pight, Henry, 1678
Platt, Thomas, 1619
Porter, Luke, 1679
Powell, Ralph, 1621
Priest, Peter, 1667
Pritchard, Polydore, 1649
Procter, Francis, 1631
Pycroft, Walter, 1624

I. R., 1676
N. R., 1679
O. R., 1676
Rack, Charles, 1691
Randall, Lewis, 1609
Raper, Christopher, 1694
Rawlins, William, 1668
Reade, Simon, 1660
Redding, Theodore, 1687
Redhead, Anthony, 1695
Redhead, Gabriel, 1689
Relfe, Edward, 16—
Renton, John. 1687
Reynolds, Thos., 1669
Ricroft, Walter, 1622
Ridding, Theophilus, 1679
Ridding, Thomas, 1697
Roaffe, George, 1600
Roberts, Oliver, 1644
Roberts, William, 1618
Robins, John, 1638
Royston, Ambrose, 1609
Royston, ———, 1620

Rudd, Anthony, 1629
Rudsby, Andrew, 1692
Russell, Thomas, 1611

I. S., 1685
R. S., 1669
T. S., 1663
Scott, Benj., 1656
Seabright, Charles, 1685
Seddon, Charles, 1669
Seears, Roger, 1651
Seeling, John, 1656
Shackle, Thos., 1686
Shath, Thos., 1680
Sheppard, Robt., 1619
Sherman, Richard, 1693
Shurmes, Richard, 1641
Siar, William, 1640
Silk, John, 1658
Simkin, James, 1659
Singleton, Lewis, 1615
Skinn, John, 1679
Skinner, John, 1670
Smackergill, Wm., 1610
Smalpiece, Rich., 16—
Smite, George, 1672
Smith, George, 1623
Smith, John, 1656
Smith, Thomas, 1669
Smith (2), Thomas, 1689
Smithe, Thomas, 1631
Smyth, Geo., 1660
Snow, Samuel, 1681
Staples, Richard, 1623
Steventon, Richard, 1608
Steward, John, 1600
Steward (2), John, 1634
Steward, John, 1641
Steward, Rowland, 1694
Steward, Thomas, 1692

Steward, Toby, 1630
Stone, Howard, 1698
Stribblehill, Thos., 1693
Sturt, Walter, 1679
Sweeting, Charles, 1658
Sweeting (2), Charles, 1685
Sweeting, Henry, 1646
Sweeting, John, 1661

H. T., 1680
I. T., 1698
R. T., 1668
Taylor, Abraham, 1651
Taudin, James, 1679
Teale, John, 1690
Templeman, Thomas, 1697
Thorogood, Nicholas, 1634
Titterton, Robert, 1698
Tough, Charles, 1667
Tough (2), Charles, 1689
Turner, Nicholas, 1606
Turner, Stephen, 1694

W. V., 1078
Vernon, Rich., 1650
Vile, Thomas, 1675
Vincent, John, 1685

A. W., 1698
R. W., 1692
R. W., 1677
W. W., 1662
Walker, John, 1617
Webb, Christopher, 1669
Webb, Richard, 1699
Westcott, Henry, 1640
Wetwood, Katherine, 1633
Whitaker, Benj., 16—
White, Joseph, 1658

Wiggin, Henry, 1690
Willett, Richard, 1666
Winchcombe, Thomas. 1697
Withebed, Richard, 1678
Withers, William, 1667

Witter, Samuel, 1682
Wood, John, 1612
Woodford, John, 1669
Woodward, Robert, 1699
Wycherley, Thos., 1626

FROM 1700 TO 1800

Abbott, Thomas, 1792
Ackland, Thomas, 1728
Alderson, John, 1771
Alderwick, Richard, 17—
Allanson, Edward, 1702
Allen, James, 1740
Ames, Thomas, 17—
Appleton, Henry, 1751
Appleton, John, 1779
Altergood, Thomas, 1700
Atwood, William, 1736

Babb, Bernard, 17—
Bache, Richard, 17—
Bacon, George, 1746
Bacon, Thomas, 17—
Bailey, John, 1789
Bampton, William, 1785
Barber, Nathan, 1782
Barker, Joseph, 1797
Barker, Samuel, 1786
Barlow, John, 17—
Barnes, Thomas, 1738
Barron, Robt., 1786
Basnet, Nathaniel, 1777
Bathhurst, John, 1715
Bearsley, Allinson, 1711
Bearsley, Job, 1711
Beaumont, W., 17—
Beckett, Thos., 1715
Beckon, Thos., 17—

Beeston, Geo., 1756
Belson, John, 1748
Bemsley, Edward, 1749
Bennett & Chapman, 17—
Bennett, Thomas, 17—
Benson, John, 1740
Bishop, James, 17—
Blake, John, 1783
Bland, John, 1734
Blenman, John, 17—
Boardman, Thomas, 1746
Boos, Samuel, 1715
Boost, James, 1758
Borman, Robt., 1701
Boteter, John, 1748
Bourchier, Cleeve, 1736
Bowley, Henry, 17—
Box, Edward, 1745
Bradstreet, Richard, 17—
Brick & Villars, 1747
Bromfield, John, 17—
Brown, Richard, 1731
Brown & Swanson, 17—
Broxup, Rich., 1793
Buckby, Thomas, 1716
Budden, David, 17—
Bullock, James, 1752
Bullock (2), James, 1758
Burford, Thos., 1779
Burford & Green, 17—
Burges, Thos., 17—
Buttery, Thos., 17—

I. C., 1723
Caney, Jos., 1748
Carpenter, Henry, 1786
Carpenter, John, 1739
Carpenter & Hamberers, 17—
Carter, Sam'l, 1794
Cartwright, Thos., 1745
Cator, John, 1752
Chamberlain, Thos., 1765
Charlesby, Wm., 1764
Chawner, Wm., 1761
Child, Lawrence, 1702
Clack, Richard, 1754
Claridge, Charles, 1758
Claridge, Joseph, 1739
Clark, John, 1788
Clark, Thomas, 1711
Clarke, Samuel, 1732
Clarke, William, 1750
Clarke & Greening, 17—
Cleeve, Alex., 1719
Cleve, Edward, 1743
Clements, John, 1782
Cole, Richard, 17—
Collett, Thos., 1737
Collier, Richard, 1737
Collins, Sam'l, 1768
Cooch, Wm., 1782
Cook, Wm., 1707
Cooke & Freeman, 17—
Cooke, Edw., 1701
Cotton, Jonathan, 1750
Cotton (2), Jonathan, 1759
Cotton, Thomas, 1778
Cowley, John, 1736
Cowley, Wm., 1734
Cowling, Wm., 17—
Cox, Wm., 17—
Cripps, Mark, 1762
Crossfield, Robt., 1707

Cudley, Robt., 17—
Curd, Thos., 1756

T. D., 1732
Darling, Thos., 1758
Davis, John, 1747
Deane, Robert, 17—
De Jersey, Wm., 1773
Digges, Wm., 17—
Dodson, Thomas, 1775
Donne, John, 1727
Donne, Joseph, 1740
Dove, John, 1713
Drinkwater, Richard, 17—
Durand, Jonas, 1726
Durand (2), Jonas, 1763
Dyer, John, 1703
Dyer, Lawrence, 1726

I. E., 1714
Eden, William, 1737
Edwards, John, 17—
Egan, Andrew, 1783
Elderton, John, 1731
Ellicott, Barth, 17—
Elliot, ———, 1746
Ellis, John, 1770
Ellis, Samuel, 1748
Ellis, William, 17—
Ellwood, Wm., 1733
Elwick, Henry, 17—
Emes, John, 1700
Emmerton, Thos., 1736
Engley, Arthur, 17—
Evat, Thos., 1797
Ewsters, Thomas, 1753

Farmer, John, 1736
Farson, John, 1745
Fasson, John, 1762

Fasson, Wm., 1787
Field, Edward, 1771
Fieldar, Henry, 17—
Fletcher, Richard, 1701
Floyd, John, 1787
Fly, Timothy, 1739
Fly & Thompson, 1740
Fontain, James, 1786
Ford, Abram, 1719
Ford, John, 1772
Foster, John, 17—
Franklyn, Richard, 1730
Frith, Thomas, 17—
Fryer, John, 1710

I. G., 1765
Gale, Rich., 17—
Giffin, Thomas, 1766
Giles, Wm., 1769
Gillam, Everard, 17—
Glover & Annison, 17—
Goater, Thos., 1758
Gooch, William, 17—
Grant, Edward, 1741
Green, Jas., 1778
Green, Wm., 1737
Greenwood, Thos., 17—
Grendon, Daniel, 1700
Grigg, Sam'l, 17—
Groce, Thos., 17—
Groves, Edmund, 1773
Grunwin, Rich., 1729
Gwilt, 1709
Gwyn, Bacon, 1709

H. H., 1709
W. H., 1709
Hagshaw, Rich., 17—
Hammerton, Henry, 1733

Hamond, Geo., 1709
Hancock, Samuel, 1714
Handy, Wm., 1746
Harris, Jabez, 1734
Harrison, Wm., 17—
Hasselborne, Jacob, 1722
Hawkins, Thomas, 17—
Hayton, John, 17—
Healy, William, 17—
Heath, John, 1720
Herne, Daniel, 1767
Highmore, Wm., 1742
Higley, Samuel, 17—
Hinde, John, 1796
Hislopp, Rich., 17—
Hitchins, John, 1786
Hitchman, James, 1716
Hitchman (2), James, 1761
Hoare, Thos., 1728
Holley, John, 1706
Holman, Ary, 1790
Holmes, George, 1746
Home, John, 1771
Hone, Wm., 1713
Hosier, Joseph, 1700
Howard, Wm., 1702
Hubbard, Robt., 1717
Hudson, John, 17—
Hulls, John, 1709
Hulls, Wm., 1744
Hume, Geo., 17—
Hutchins, Wm., 1732
Hux, Thomas, 1739
Hux, William, 1728

F. I., 1713
I. I., 1700
Iles, John, 1709
Iles, Nath., 1719
Iles, Robt., 1735

Jackman, Nicholas, 1735
Jackson, John, 1712
Jackson (2), John, 1731
James, Anthony, 1713
Jeffreys, Joseph, 17—
Jeffreys, Sam'l, 1739
Jenner, A., 1700
Jennings, Theodore, 1741
Johnson, Luke, 1723
Johnson & Chamberlain, 17—
Jones, Clayton, 1746
Jones, John, 1750
Jones, Seth, 17—
Joseph, Henry, 1771
Jupe, John, 1761
Jupe, Robt., 1737

T. K., 1709
Kendrick, John, 1754
Kent, John, 1749
Kenton, John, 1711
King, Joseph, 1709
King, Richard, 1746
King (2), Richard, 1796
King, Robt., 1711
King, W. H., 1786

Laffar, John, 1720
Lamb, Joseph, 1738
Langford, John, 1757
Langley, John, 17—
Law, Sam'l, 1700
Lawrence, Edw., 17—
Lawrence, John, 1723
Lawson, Daniel, 17—
Leach, Jonathan, 17—
Leach, Thomas, 1747
Leapidge, Edw., 1724
Leapidge, Thos., 1763
Leggatt, James, 1755

Leggatt, R., 1746
Lindsay, J., 17—
Little, Henry, 1755
Loader, Chas., 17—
Lockwood, Edw., 1790
Long, William, 1707

N. M., 1782
Mart, John, 17—
Masham, Hugh, 1713
Massam, Robt., 1740
Mathews, Edw., 1728
Mathews, James, 1746
Mathews, Philip, 1743
Mathews, Wm., 1741
Maxey, Chas., 1752
Maxted, Henry, 17—
Meadows, Wm., 17—
Meakin, Nath., 1768
Merefield, Ed., 17—
Middleton, Leon, 1752
Miles, Wm., 17—
Millin, Wm., 1786
Mitchell, John, 1755
Morse, Robt., 1709
Moulins, Robt., 1704
Moxon, Samuel, 1799
Mudge, Walter, 1793
Munday, Thos., 1767
Munden, Wm., 1771
Murray, Wm., 17—

Nash, Edw., 1738
Newham, John, 1731
Newham, Wm., 1727
Nettlefold, Wm., 1799
Newman, Rich., 1753
Nicholls, Thomas, 1786
Nicholson, Jas., 1730
Nicholson, Robt., 1725

Norfolk, Jos., 1764
Norfolk, Rich., 1776
North, George, 1703

O'Neal, Richard, 1728
Osborne, John, 1715
Oudley, Robt., 1725

H. P., 1707
T. P., 1700
Padden, Thomas, 1705
Pandal, John, 17—
Parker, Dan, 1710
Parr, Robt., 1767
Partridge, Richard, 17—
Patience, Robt., 1772
Pattison, Simon, 1733
Pawson, Richard, 17—
Peacock, Samuel, 1785
Peacock, Thomas, 1783
Peake, Richard, 1700
Peircy, Robert, 1760
Peisley, George, 1719
Peisley, Thomas, 17—
Pender, Charles, 17—
Perchard, Hellier, 1745
Perchard, Sam'l, 1752
Perry, John, 1773
Peter, John, 1714
Phillips, Wm., 1783
Phipps, Wm., 17—
Pidgwin, John, 1785
Piggott, Francis, 1770
Piggott, John, 1738
Piggott, Thomas, 1725
Pilkington, Robt., 1709
Pitt, Richard, 1781
Pitt & Dadley, 1780
Pitt & Floyd, 178-
Pole, Robt., 1748

Poole, Richard, 1746
Porteous, Robt., 1790
Porteous, Thos., 1765
Powell, Thos., 1706
Pratt, Joseph, 1720
Price, John, 1781
Priddle, Samuel, 1798
Prince, John, 17—
Puleston, James, 17—
Pullen, Sam'l, 1714

Quick, Edward, 1756
Quick (2), Edward, 1772
Quick, Hugh, 1708

J. E. R., 178-
Raindell, Charles, 17—
Randall, Edward, 1711
Read, Isaac, 17—
Redknap, Peter, 1720
Reynolds, Robt., 1767
Rhodes, Thos., 1746
Richards, Timothy, 17—
Ridding, Joseph, 1735
Ridgley, Wm., 1731
Righton, Samuel, 1737
Roberts, Philip, 1753
Robins, James, 1725
Rogers, Phillip, 17—
Rolt, John, 17—
Rooke, Richard, 1777
Rose, Samuel, 1701
Rowles, Thomas, 1732
Rudsey, Andrew, 17--

I. S., 1703
I. S., 1726
W. S., 1706
Sandys, Wm., 1703
Savage, John, 1741

Savage (2), John, 1758
Scarlet, Thos., 1765
Scatchard, Robert, 1761
Scattergood, Thos., 1733
Seabroke, Robert, 1794
Seawell, Edward, 1797
Sellon, John, 17—
Sewdley, Henry, 1738
Shackle, Thos., 1701
Sharrock, Edmund, 1742
Sharwood, James, 1776
Shaw, James, 1796
Sheppard, Thos., 17—
Sherwin, Joseph, 17—
Shorey, Barth, 1747
Shorey, John, 1711
Shorey (2), John, 1720
Sidby, Edw., 17—
Silk, John, 1700
Skynmer, Robert, 17—
Slaughter, Richard, 1742
Smalley, Sam'l, 1701
Smallman, Arthur, 17—
Smith, Anthony, 1702
Smith, Charles, 1789
Smith, Geo., 1795
Smith, John, 1709
Smith, Joseph, 1706
Smith, Richard, 1705
Smith, Sam'l, 1753
Smith, William, 1799
Smith & Leapidge, 1750
Snape, William, 17—
Spackman, Jas., 1742
Spackman, Joseph, 1761
Spackman & Co., 1765
Spackman & Grant, 176—
Sparrow, Francis, 1746
Spateman, Sam'l, 1750
Spooner, Rich., 1749

Spring, Penry, 17—
Spring, Thomas, 1720
Stafford, Geo., 1740
Stanley, Francis, 1722
Starkey, Joseph, 1748
Steevens, James, 1754
Stevens, James, 1774
Stevens, Philip, 1716
Stevens, Thos., 1732
Stevens, William, 1710
Stiles, John, 1730
Stout, Alex., 17—
Strong, Francis, 1746
Sturton, Anthony, 1702
Summers, John, 1747
Swanson, Thomas, 1777
Sweeting, Chas., 1717

Taylor, Geo., 1783
Taylor, Sam'l, 1748
Taylor, Thos., 1704
Thomas, Walter, 1756
Thompson, Thos., 17—
Thompson, William, 1738
Tidmarsh, James, 1750
Tidmarsh, Thos., 1721
Tilyard, John, 1752
Tisoe, James, 1764
Tisoe, John, 1774
Toms, Edward, 1783
Tonkin, Mathew, 1749
Townsend, John, 1748
Townsend & Compton, 1750
Trahern, Edw., 1712
Tribblewell, Thos., 17—
Tumberville, Dawbeny, 1714

Ubly, Edward, 1727
Ubly, Thos., 1751
Underwood, Mathew, 1752

G. V., 1712
Vaughn, John, 1792

I. W., 1715
W. W., 1721
Walmsley, John, 1712
Warkman, Rich., 1727
Watson, Joseph, 17—
Watterer, Thos., 1709
Watts, John, 1760
Watts (2) John, 1780
Webb, Joseph, 1726
Webb, Thomas, 17—
Welford, James, 1754
Welford, John, 1788
Westwood, Joseph, 1706
Wheeler, Thos., 17—
White, Rich., 1729
White & Bernard, 17—
White, Wm., 1743
Whittle, Francis, 1731
Wiggins, Abram, 17—

Wilks, Rich., 17—
Willey, Mary, 17—
Williams, John, 17—
Wingood, John, 1766
Wingood, Joseph, 1767
Winter, George, 17—
Withers, Benj., 1730
Wood, Henry, 1786
Wood, Robt., 1701
Wood, Wm., 1744
Wood & Hill, 17—
Wood & Mitchell, 17—
Woodeson, John, 17—
Wright, John, 1743
Wright, Joseph, 17—
Wright, Wm., 1772
Wynn, John, 1763

Yates, Lawrence, 1757
Yates, Rich., 1783
Yewen, John, 17—
Yorke, Edw., 1772

FROM 1800 TO 1847

Alderson, Geo., 1817
Arden, John, 1821
Ashley, James, 1824
Ashley, T. J. T., 1824

Bache, Richard, 1804
Bagshaw, Richard, 1809
Bagshaw, Thomas, 1810
Barnett, Robt., 1815
Basnett, John, 1821
Bathhurst, John, 1800
Blake, John, 1832
Bowring, Chas., 1820
Burt, Andrew, 1802

Carter, Jos., 1812

Cocks, Sam'l, 1819
Collins, Dan'l, 1805
Collins (2), Dan'l, 1812
Collins, Jas., 1811
Compton, Thos., 1807
Cooper, Geo., 1819
Cooper, Rich., 1818
Cooper, Thos., 1838

Dackombe, Aquila, 1818
Dadley, Edwd., 1804

Fasson, Benj., 1815
Fasson, Thos., 1803
Field, Dan'l S., 1830
Fisher, Paul, 18—

Gibbs, Wm., 18—
Godfrey, Jos. Hen., 18—
Grainge, John, 1816
Grattan, Joseph, 1839
Groome, Wm., 18—

Hall, John, 1810
Hall (2), John, 1823
Hinde, John, 1800
Hodge, Robt. P., 1802
Hudson, John, 1804
Hurst, Richard, 1826

Jackson, R., 1801
Joseph, Rich., 1805

Mister, Rich., 1827
Morning, Randall, 1821
Moser, Roger, 1806
Mourgue, Fulcrand, 1807
Mullens, John, 1805

Palmer, Ebenezer, 1818
Palmer, Rich., 1822
Parker, Wm., 1809

Perry, John, 1808
Phillips, John, 1815
Phillips, Thos., 1817
Pierce, Jas. H., 1825
Potter, George, 1831

Reeve, John, 1818
Reeve, Joseph, 1807
Reeve, Wm., 1833
Robinson, G., 1808
Robinson (2), G., 1818
Ruffin, Thomas, 1808

Sansbry, Wm., 1810
Smith, Isaac, 1813
Stanton, Robt., 1818
Staples, Henry, 1817

Taylor, Ebenezer, 1847
Toulmin, Geo., 1805
Tovey, Wm., 1801
Towers, ———, 1807
Towers, ———, 1809

Weaver, Wm., 1801

SCOTTISH PEWTERERS

FROM 1600 TO 1700

Abernethie, Wm., 1649
Andersone, Robt., 1697

Borthwick, Andrew, 1620
Bowal, Robt., 1621
Bryce, Jas., 1654
Burnbell, Robt., 1633
Burns, Robt., 1694

Christie, Wm., 1652

Cortyne, Thos., 1630
Coutie, Wm., 1619

Edgar, Thos., 1654
Edgar, Robt., 1684
Gledstane, Geo. (1), 1610
Gledstane, Geo. (2), 1634
Gowat, Robt., 1621
Graham, Alexr., 1654
Guld, John, 1677

Hamiltone, Wm., 1630
Harvie, John, 1643
Harvie, Jas., 1654
Harvie, Wm. (^{1}), 1672
Hernie, Jas., 1651
Herrin, Jas., 1686
Herrin, Jas., 1692
Herrin, John, 1686
Hunter, Alex., 1682

Inglis, Robt., 1663
Inglis, Thos. (^{1}), 1621
Inglis, Thos. (^{2}), 1647
Inglis, Thos. (^{3}), 1686

Lyndsay, Alex., 1648

Moir, Wm., 1675
Monteith, Jas. (^{1}), 1634
Monteith, Jas. (^{2}), 1643
Munro, Andr., 1677

Napier, John, 1666

Penman, Wm., 1693

Ramsay, John, 1659

Scott, John, 1621
Sibbald, Alex., 1613
Sibbald, Jas., 1631
Simpsone, Robt., 1631
Somervell, Jas., 1616
Syde, John, 1680
Symountson, Jas., 1696

Thompsone, Gilbert, 1669

Walker, Jas., 1643
Walker, Patrick, 1607
Walker (^{2}), Patrick, 1637
Walker, Robt., 1676
Watson, John, 1671
Weir, Robt., 1646
Weir, Thos., 1631
Whyte, Geo., 1676

FROM 1700 TO 1800

Affleck, Jas., 1741
Affleck, Robt., 1741
Andersone, Adam, 1747

Ballantine, John, 1755
Brown, John, 1761
Bruce, John, 1749
Burton, Mungo, 1709
Bunkell, Ed., 1720

Chalmer, Roedrick, 1750
Clarkson, James, 1717
Clerk, Jas., 1721
Cockburn, Thos., 1711

Coultard, Alex., 1708
Coulter, Wm., 1751
Cowper, Jas., 1704
Cunninghame, Wm., 1740
Cuthbert, John, 1712

Drum, Geo., 1740

Edgar, Jas., 1709
Erskine, Alex., 1770

Finlay, Robt., 17—
Fleming, Wm., 17—
Folly, John, 1714
Fraser, Simon, 1740

Gardiner, ——, 1764
Gibson, ——, 1719
Gourlay, David, 1800
Grier, John, 1701

Harvie, Wm., 1706
Herdrig, Thomas, 1741
Hunter, William, 1749

Kello, Robt., 1715
Kinbrick, John, 17—
Kininburgh, Robt., 1794
Kinnear, Alex., 1750

Letham, John, 1718
Lockhart, James, 1792

Mitchell, Hugh, 1720
Mitchell, Thos., 1705
Monteith, James, 1767

Nail, Thos., 1792
Napier, John, 1700

Paterson, Walter, 1710
Peddie, Andrew, 1766
Prentice, Robt., 1781

Rait, John, 1718
Reid, Robt., 1718

Scott, Wm., 1794
Simpson, Thomas, 1728
Stewart, Thomas, 1781

Tait, Adam, 1747
Tait, John, 1700
Tait (2), John, 1747
Tennent, Geo., 1706

Waddel, Alex., 1714
Weir, John, 1701
Wilsone, John, 1732
Wright, Alex., 1732
Wright, James, 1780

SOME AMERICAN PEWTERERS

Richard Graves, 1639, Boston, Mass.
Henry Shrimpton, 1660, Boston, Mass.
James Leddel, 1744, Sign of the Platter, New York
Robert Boyle, 1755, Sign of the Dish, New York
Francis Bassett, 1786-1799, Queen and Pearl Sts., New York
William Kirkby, 1786-1792, Great Dock and Old Slip, New York
Henry Will, 1786, Water St., New York
Thomas Badger, 1789, Prince St., Boston
Thomas Green, 1789, Dock Square, Boston
Joseph Roby, 1789, Three doors of Drawbridge, Boston
Frederick Bassett, 1792-1798, Pearl St., New York
George Coldwell, 1792-1808, Gold St., New York
William Elsworth, 1792, Courtlandt St., New York

Robert Pearse, 1792, Chatham St., New York
Richard Austen, 1796, Marlboro St., Boston
John Skinner, 1796, Newbury St., Boston
John Welch, 1796, Union St., Boston
Malcom M'Ewen & Son, 1794, Beekman Slip, New York
Michel André, 1796, 255 Broadway, New York
George Youle, 1798-1821, Water St., New York
Philip, Fields, 1799, Bowery Lane, New York
Moses Lafetra, 1812-1816, Beekman St., New York
Anthony Allaire, 1815-1821, Hester St., New York
Lafetra & Allaire, 1816, Water St., New York
Thomas Youle, 1816, Water St., New York
James Bird, 1820, Harman St., New York
Widow Youle (of Thomas), 1821, Water St., New York
Boardman & Co., 1824, Water St., New York
Boardman & Hart, 1828-1841, Water St., New York
    (Later they moved to 6 Burling Slip, and made block tin and
    Britannia ware.)
Thomas Wildes, 1832-1840, Hester and Second Sts., New York
George Richardson, 1825, Oliver Place, Boston
Homans & Co., Cincinnati, O.
Padelford & Palenthorpe, Philadelphia, Pa.

INDEX

INDEX

PAGES

223

INDEX

227

PAGES

Mazer bowls	61
Measures	60
"Memorials of London"	36
McEwen, Malcolm	112
Middle Ages	4
Montayne, Abram	129
Mont St. Michel	16
Monumental brasses	118–120
Moulds for pewter	33, 34, 40
Nelson, Lord	190, 191
"New England Rarities"	77
"New England's Prospect"	133
Noggin	66
Nuremberg	10, 19, 20
"Old English Plate"	64, 65
"Old West Surrey"	73, 74
Oxford	125
Palimpsests	119
"Paston Letters"	43, 44
Pearsall, Nathaniel	163
Penton, G.	144
Pewterers' Hall	38, 46
Pewter pots	19
"Philocothonista"	58
Pie-coffins	61
Pins	121–123
Pipkins	143
"Pirley Pig"	91
Plates	34
Porringers	9
Posnets	67
Pottle-pot	59
Price list	113, 114
Pricked work	23
Purling, Major	51
Quaich	91
Queen Anne	58, 74

INDEX

229

PAGES

Thimbles	146
Tin	6, 7, 19, 32, 33, 37, 39
Tips	147
Tokens	15, 16, 92, 93
Tools	23, 35, 177
Touch-marks	46, 49–51
"Triflers"	38
"Vessels of tin"	37
Warming-pans	162–164
Washington, General	105, 122, 127, 144, 163
Washington, Mrs.	105, 107–109, 122
Weight of vessels	53, 54, 58–60
Welch, Charles	35
Whale oil	77, 78
Whipple House	133
White metal	69
Will, Henry	112
Winslow, Edward	161
Woking	157
"Worshipful Company of Pewterers"	35–41, 49, 50, 55–60, 71, 80–84
"Wriggled work"	21
Wright, Lemuel	123
Yeomanry	56
York	139